Towards a Living Church
Family and Community Catechesis

Towards
a Living Church

Family and Community
Catechesis

WIM SARIS SDB

COLLINS

Collins Liturgical Publications
187 Piccadilly, London W1V 9DA

Originally published as *Daar Gebeurt
Kerk 1. Gezinskatechese*, © Uitgeverij
Stichting Don Bosco, Holland.

Translation into English by Eileen Hurley.
Additional sections translated by Ines Ceruti.
© English translation
The Southern African Catholic Bishops'
Conference, PO Box 941, Pretoria 0001,
South Africa.

Nihil obstat : Paul Nadal
Imprimatur : + Denis E. Hurley OMI
Archbishop of Durban

ISBN 0 00 599644 9
First published this edition 1980

Typeset by Texet, Leighton Buzzard, Beds.
Made and printed in Great Britain by
William Collins Sons & Co. Ltd. Glasgow

CONTENTS

Foreword, Editorial Board   7

Introduction   11

Acknowledgements   13

PART I RELIGIOUS EDUCATION PAST AND PRESENT

1. Religious education requires teamwork   18
2. New pastoral offer   24
3. Family catechesis   26
4. Equipping   29

PART II   CATECHESIS OF LIFE

5. Realistic catechesis   38
6. Meditative catechesis   43
7. Formation catechesis   48
8. Relationship catechesis   54
9. Sacramental catechesis   71
10. Catechesis and science   79

PART III   THE COMMUNION PROJECT

11. The time is ripe   94
12. Helping each other to decide   100
13. The motivation   104
14. Starting early   108
15. The parents' evening   110
16. Working it out in practice   115
17. Internal division of tasks   123
18. Project and process   131

PART IV EDUCATORS IN THE FAITH

19. Not 'playing school'   142
20. Act first, then talk   146
21. The first milieu of faith   149
22. The second milieu of faith   156
23. The Sunday liturgy   159
24. Interaction   165
25. Task sharing and teamwork   170
26. Family catechesis: a summing up   181

Table I: Catechesis and science   80
Table II: Family catechesis as a pastoral project and process   132
Table III: Task sharing and teamwork   171

Appendix I: An alternative cycle for the Communion Project
    in the Southern Hemisphere   186

Index   189

FOREWORD

Family catechesis originated in a small group of five parishes in Amsterdam South. The enthusiastic response of the two hundred families who took part became infectious. In 1973 the number of participants grews to 1,400 in twenty different parishes, mainly in and around Amsterdam. In 1974 it spread to Alkmaar and Haarlem and the provinces of Holland. By 1975 it had become known throughout Holland. Because of its inner vitality it spreads naturally and leads to the involvement of people. At present Southern Africa and Belgium are showing keen interest. This book has also been translated into Italian.

The author, Wim Saris, is a Salesian of Don Bosco who has had many years experience in religious education and youth work in schools and parishes. As co-ordinator of youth work he searched for new ways and means of developing a pastoral offer which would affect old and young alike. When Wim Saris was appointed Dean of Amsterdam South the way was open for him to combine catechesis and pastoral work as a total pastoral offer in the form of family catechesis. In this book he gives a practical and clear explanation of this approach against the background of the Dutch Church moving towards renewal.

This is the official English translation of Wim Saris' book on Family Catechesis, *Daar Gebeurt Kerk*, with additions and revisions suggested by the author. In it he describes the origins and development of Family Catechesis and explains in some detail the principles on which this approach is based (Parts I and II). He also includes a description of a Communion Project (Part III), showing how to put the theory into practice. Throughout, Saris shares his experiences and those of his team and honestly sets forth the difficulties as well as the successes that have accompanied the growth of Family Catechesis. He situates this approach to catechesis within the total context of education and outlines the specific roles, the priorities and interaction of the partners in religious education — the family, the school and the Church (Part IV).

This book will be of interest to pastors, teachers, catechists — all who are called to promote lay involvement in the growth of Christian communities at parish or diocesan level. It can be regarded as a manual to accompany the Communion Project File, which is available in English in Southern Africa. In addition, it will be of interest to the adult believer to whom it offers a deeper insight into his role and responsibility in the Church today. In this context, it may also be of value to other Christian communions.

There are a number of points to which the translators would like to draw attention:

1. For the purpose of this book the term "Family Catechesis" has a *specialised* meaning. It is not to be confused with home-centred catechesis or programmes involving parents at home in formal catechesis. To stress this the English translation uses the term *"Family and Community Catechesis"*.

2. Two contrasting technical terms are frequently used:
   a) Total context (*totaal konteks*) and
   b) Part-process (*deel processes*)
   a) *Total context* refers to a holistic concept of religious education—the home, the school and the parish. Family and community catechesis draws attention to the respective roles of the partners in religious education and advocates a total approach.
   b) *Part-process* education, on the other hand, refers to any one of the three partners in the total context. So, formal catechesis would be regarded as a part-process in the total context of religious education.

3. The term *pastor* used throughout this book is not necessarily to be identified with the term *priest*, but must be understood as implying any official office bearer in the Church: catechist, lay theologian, deacon, priest.

4. The cycle Saris offers in his Communion Project (p. 120) follows the seasons in the Northern Hemisphere and coincides with the Liturgical Year. An alternative plan for the Southern Hemisphere is provided (Appendix I).

5. Even though this book is written from a situation in which the third partner in religious education is the Catholic school, its

8

thesis applies equally where formal religious education is provided by parish catechesis.

6. Inherent in the whole concept of Family Catechesis is its need for adaptation to local communities and circumstances.

7. In order to implement what is suggested in this book, the Communion Project File is necessary.

Editorial Board
Family and Community Catechesis
for Southern Africa

INTRODUCTION

Family Catechesis was born of the crisis which modern catechesis and pastoral work are experiencing at the present time: that they cannot get across to, cannot affect or strike root among the vast masses — the ordinary faithful. The great majority of ordinary people were not so poor in faith ten or twenty years ago, but many of them now have the feeling that their religion has been taken away from them. Obviously, nobody intended that this should happen. But they just cannot keep up with what has been dropped, changed and renewed. All this happened over their heads. And in spite of material progress and prosperity, there has been a great increase in the number of poor — the poor in faith.

Family catechesis brings the faith back to where it belongs in the first place: to the family. It gives parents back the faith, and the responsibility of living out this faith in their own family circle, at their own level. Unless parents are approached as completely worthy and equal partners, every higher form of pastoral care, of liturgical renewal or catechesis will lack roots. Family catechesis is essential here. For this reason it has well been called the missing link in catechesis and pastoral work.

The communion project offers an invitation to parents, and equips them to live a genuine personal faith with their children once again. In the normal course of events this process should have been going on for at least eight years or more. *Towards a Living Church* provides the background to the communion project as well as a number of helpful suggestions. A further book is planned, to give the background and suggestions related to the confirmation project.

Wim Saris SDB

ACKNOWLEDGEMENTS

The Editorial Board for Family and Community Catechesis for Southern Africa wishes to place on record its gratitude to the following:

To Fr. Wim Saris SDB, the initiator of Family Catechesis, for his kind permission to translate and publish his book *Daar Gebeurt Kerk* in English and for suggesting revisions to his original text which are incorporated in this translation.

To the Southern African Catholic Bishops' Conference and, in particular, Archbishop Denis Hurley OMI, Chairman of the Commission for Christian Education and Worship, for their support and encouragement.

To Miss Eileen Hurley for her dedicated service in translating the book.

To Miss Ines Ceruti of the Grail who translated the revised sections and who organised the typing of the manuscript.

To the photographers: Fr. Luke Mettler CMM; Mr Michael Shinners; Mr Trevor Lotter.

To the many typists who offered their services voluntarily during various stages in the editing.

Finally, the Chairman, Editor and Secretary of the Editorial Board would like to express their admiration and appreciation of their Technical Advisor Fr. Kees Keijsper OP who introduced Family Catechesis to Southern Africa and accompanied its development to its present stage. Thanks to his perseverance, Family and Community Catechesis has been adopted as an official catechetical programme by the Commission for Christian Education and Worship of the Southern African Catholic Bishops' Conference.

Pretoria
31 January 1979
Feast of Saint John Bosco

13

Photo: Luke Mettler

PART I
RELIGIOUS EDUCATION PAST AND PRESENT

*Relationships between
people are of far more
importance than all the
"know how" in the world—
they are of vital importance.
The latest insights are of no
use to young people if they
cut them off from the vital
ties of love and happiness.*

Photo: Luke Mettler

A novel often begins by relating how well the partners get on together. Then follows the estrangement and very soon it looks as though it is all over between them. Fortunately there is a turning point and the main characters find each other again, now somewhat the wiser. What we are about to say about the partners in religious education follows much the same pattern.

* Religious education requires team-work. It takes place in a total context. At one time this was the Catholic circle. And within that context the Catholic school educated children for the Catholic Church. But now this pattern has been shattered. At present the school is seeking its own way. For this reason, parents and parishes feel somewhat left out in the cold. We are seeking new pastoral methods, in order to promote team-work in religious education for the sake of sound education in the schools and elsewhere (p. 18).

* A new pastoral approach must not take its conclusions as starting points, but must begin where people are. If we are serious in saying that parents are primarily responsible for their children's religious education, then we must draw up a scheme which they can really use in their family. That is the purpose of family catechesis (p. 24).

* Family catechesis is a service rendered by the parish. It is a parish catechesis for parents which is so practical that it immediately becomes an integral part of their lives and begins to function as a catechesis for children through the family, simply by the way they live (p. 26).

* Family catechesis is concerned with equipping parents to play their part. It is not a course, it simply helps them to pose their own questions and to live the religious dimension of their own lives more consciously. This happens as a process of interaction among all who take part — old and young. Parents feel themselves confirmed in their role of responsibility. This is an indirect form of adult catechesis that is less threatening and therefore more fruitful (p. 29).

In human relationships,
a one-sided approach
always alienates.

1. RELIGIOUS EDUCATION REQUIRES TEAMWORK

Believing is a special way of looking — of looking at everything: at life, the world, one's own existence — with the conviction that all of these are 'in God' and have their place in him. Faith is that dimension of man which is essential to his wholeness as a person. It affects all aspects of his life and behaviour. Religious education for the young can therefore only be effective if it has a place in the total context which includes àll aspects, participants and relationships in that young life — his family members, the believing community, the school community and the young person himself.

Within the catholic circle

In the past the total context consisted of the immediate environment of the particular Catholic circle of society. Within this circle it was one's duty to send one's children to a Catholic school; everything else followed automatically from that. The task of the school was quite clear: to train children for, and to introduce them to, the world of Catholic adults. Parents were only too happy to drop their children off at the front door of the school because they knew that through the back door (or even through the connecting door) they would enter the Catholic church.

The school was an extension and instrument of the church. There the children received religious instruction on prayer, communion, confession, confirmation and, what's more, these were immediately put into practice. There seemed no danger that parents would be forced out, or would fall behind because the children used the twentieth edition of the catechism of which their parents had used the eighteenth. Whatever other topics children got to hear about were the very things which adult Catholics were currently discussing.

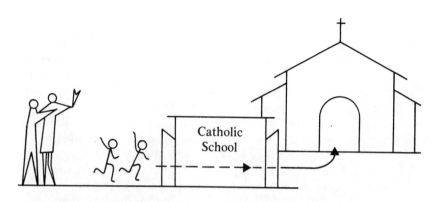

Disruption

Since then there has been a great upheaval in the pattern of society. In Catholic circles, too, many things are moving. The Church has developed an openness to the outside world. The ghetto mentality has been shattered.

At the same time, however, the secure total context has been lost. As a result part-processes which had their particular place in the old set-up and functioned within it, don't produce the same results any more. Of itself this is quite logical: if the old framework disintegrates one cannot carry on operating parts of the system without support of the whole.

One such part-process is the education of the young in the school environment. To continue to regard the school as the institution for moulding the young and fitting them to the existing order is to ask the impossible of it, because there is no longer any existing order in society or in the church. Both are in a complete state of flux. Then what should we be training the children for? For the old order which has vanished? For the new one which is not yet in existence? Does anyone know what the new order will be like?

The autonomy of the school

So within education, the question of the school's particular task, function and identity was bound to come up. This leads to an awareness that we are emerging from a state of tutelage and simultaneously reaching maturity. On principle we must ask ourselves. Are there any grounds on which we can defend the moulding of children through formal teaching to conform to structures, systems and institutions, by cramming them with information required for some kind of further education and ultimately for some job in society? Or should we be concerned primarily with the interests of the child and the optimum development of each one's unique personality and gifts in relation to his environment? For many educationalists the answer is clear: the school is an autonomous reality with a specific task. For the Catholic school this means a careful guidance of children on their way to adulthood through an education inspired by the values of the Gospel.

If we want to use the word 'Catholic' with greater precision, then we must use it not only of the institutional church but must recognise that the school too is a dimension of the living church.

The difficulty about saying that the position of the school is autonomous is that teaching is only a part-process in the total context of education. One can only talk of autonomy in the context of an education where there is good collaboration and task sharing among the partners engaged in it.

Partners out of touch

This becomes difficult, however, when one of the partners, for example the school, enters on a process of development while the other interested partners practically stand still. This is bound to cause tension and lead to conflict. In fact this is what we frequently see happening at present.

In the search for new ways, education always takes the child with it. It even puts the child at the centre. It is aiming less and less at turning out people fitted exactly to a certain mould, even though the requirements of further education and of society still play a large role. It cannot be denied that more attention is being paid to the stimulation of critical and creative thought and action. At school children learn about many things of which adults are not yet even aware. And with regard to the existing order in society, children no longer learn to accept everything passively but are taught to pose critical questions.

At home parents have no answers to these questions. They have not been prepared for them and there is in practice little or no provision for bringing parents as a group up to date. After the initial period of anxiety parents become annoyed. They had hoped that things would settle down again — the whole thing was started by a few 'leftists' anyway. This state of affairs is clearly beginning to irritate an increasing number of parents and other adults in the church and in society. To confine ourselves to our own circle: we can definitely say that many parents and parish clergy (the original partners in the framework of religious education) feel left out in the cold by present developments in the Catholic school.

Dissatisfaction

They see themselves robbed of their official educational channel to prepare the young for society and for the church. Parents are realising with shock that they can no longer follow what is happening to their children. All kinds of things are being done but, they ask, by whose authority? Meanwhile in the parish, people notice that the young have disappeared from their midst. Here and there there is great discouragement among parish clergy. They don't know any other way of reaching the youth and they feel that they are being excluded from the Catholic school. They are thinking along old lines, but they know no other lines.

And parents ask themselves — obviously along the same old lines — 'What do we have Catholic schools for?'

By means of parent-teachers' associations and in all sorts of other ways they make despairing efforts to turn back the tide so that they can once again demand traditional Catholic education from the school. But the old social pattern belongs once and for all to the past. The school rightly refers the responsibility for education in specific church practice back to the parish and to the families themselves.

Yet, in parish and family, people do not feel confident; they are not trained for it. They do not have the time for it. The truth of the matter is they are simply at a loss. In the meantime the situation keeps on developing and education grows farther away from them. So that the state of affairs becomes even more serious than before.

It is really disquieting that complaints against education are growing more and more intense. Some schools are even singled out as the main cause of the estrangement between children and parents, between youth and adults, in society and in the church. And the accusations are often levelled at the very schools which are most concerned with finding solutions suitable for our times.

It follows that reproaches, from whatever quarter, are unfair. They do not get us anywhere. There can be no question of putting the blame on any of the partners in the educational relationship. The former supportive association has fallen apart, and because of this, each party has followed a more or less autonomous process of development. Because of differences of direction and tempo we have, for the moment, grown apart from each other. But in the educational process as a whole we are continuously interacting with each other and we constantly need each other.

The solution is not for parents and the church to get the school under their thumbs again. The static total context that used to exist, under the supervision of the parish priest who was at the same time chairman of the school committee, is past. We must strive for a new dynamic total context of being together 'on the way', as equal partners, that is a total context for today based on a free and conscious choice.

It is in everybody's interest

This new total context is of the greatest importance for education and for young people. In the meantime, the developments we have mentioned have made the following things very clear:

If an educational institution and the young people it teaches drift completely apart from the other partners in the educational relationship, there is the risk of a break in the primary life-relationship of all the people involved, simply for the sake of a slight increase in the young people's store of knowledge.

People's inter-relationships are of more importance than all the 'know-how' in the world; they are of vital importance. Human happiness depends on them. They are the vital arteries of love and security, attention and acceptance, of feeling comfortable 'because you belong together'. The latest insights are no use to young people if they cut them off from living bonds and leave them isolated.

This last point is often a revelation to people. Too often parents are seen as the only victims of present-day trends. But young people also suffer. The new course of events in education and religious instruction is no help to them if the only place they can apply their insights is at school.

Let us be quite clear. I am not saying that the school is at fault in exploring new avenues. No one in education deliberately sets out to shatter relationships between young and old. But that does not alter the fact that the very things which we view as positive developments are nevertheless having just this effect on parents, pastors and parish communities. These side-effects can only be avoided when all partners keep growing at a uniform pace in their mutual relationships.

We do not solve the crisis in religious education merely by renewing school catechesis. Despite our good intentions, this just increases the estrangement between young people and their parents. A real solution to the problem of religious education can only be expected from an overall pastoral plan in which all concerned are re-equipped. Meanwhile, here and there, the part-process of school catechesis is developing quite well. The areas of family and parish catechesis still lie largely untouched. To begin with, we need a part-process of family catechesis. Later, ways can be sought to achieve good collaboration among all concerned. While it is possible to teach children something in a vacuum (even in the religious field) it is not possible to develop and educate them in a vacuum. Education occurs through people interacting. Old and young educate each other. Education is a process of growth and development of all who are involved in this specific relationship. Religious education is the same kind of relationship-occurrence. The four partners involved are the family, the church, the school and the young people themselves.

Young people are not only the object of religious education, but they are really partners in it, they have their own contribution to make, and their own responsibility towards the others.

*We do not change a
community by introducing
a conclusion of our own as
a new point of departure
for people.*

2. NEW PASTORAL OFFER

We are beginning to gain experience with the processes involved
in change. True changes do not come about through the strong
actions of pioneers, nor through men who are completely authoritarian and who walk over others; he who wishes to change people
must gradually get a complete growth and development process
going. Changing a few individuals or some circumstances within
an outmoded total context inevitably creates disorientation,
frustration and conflict. It is like new wine in old wine skins; the
skins burst and the good wine is lost. A totally new approach in
a completely outmoded situation just breaks people.

We see all these things happening in the changes that have
taken place in religious education. The statements 'parents are
primarily responsible', and 'the parish community has a particular
responsibility for the religious education of the youth in their
midst' are the statements of experts, of the few who are more
advanced in this field than the vast majority. They have come a
long way to reach these insights and conclusions. Although they
themselves are absolutely convinced, they have no right to make
these personal convictions the new starting-point for the group.
In doing so they are putting a pistol to the heads of parents and
the parish community, who have a long way to go before they
arrive at these conclusions themselves. Whoever really wishes to
renew the church community must not impose his own conclusions
as a new point of departure for the people (for example to
announce from the pulpit: From next Sunday onwards we will
receive communion in the hand — the time has come!). This is
just as authoritarian an attitude as before.

We bring about true renewal only by creating a pastoral offer
which starts from where people are and leads them to our conclusion, or maybe to another conclusion, as a point of arrival. The

approach commonly used these days understandably evokes a vehement reaction from parents suddenly confronted with the remark 'parents are primarily responsible. . .'. They experience it as a weapon used against them, because the experts themselves apparently don't know where to go next. It is a useful slogan with which to shrug off responsibility for the failure of religious education and to put the blame on the parents. One often hears it put this way: 'Now that they don't know which way to turn any more, they suddenly shove the responsibility on to us.' That 'suddenly' is extremely significant. It means that the parents were not expecting it. They feel a pistol at their heads. They have not had the opportunity of growing into the conclusion. No one has ever asked them if they are in agreement with it. Moreover they do not know what to do. They are themselves full of doubts and do not consider themselves sufficiently informed in religious matters to be able to cope with a communion project which is simply dumped on their doorsteps. When we pastors come to the conclusion that 'parents are primarily responsible', and we earnestly believe it ourselves, then there is only one thing to do: make a pastoral offer at grass-root level along the lines of FAMILY CATECHESIS which will motivate these parents, however unprepared, to take their task in hand. But then we must know how to support and equip them so that they will be in a position to carry out the task with some measure of success. Nor should we expect parents to perform tasks which are not part of family education, for example tasks which are peculiar to the believing community of the school.

*Family catechesis is a
catechesis TO adults which
in turn becomes catechesis
FROM these adults
themselves to their children.*

3. FAMILY CATECHESIS

Because of the upheavals and changes of our times many people are experiencing difficulties. It is the task of the church to understand this crisis and to be sensitive to it. In the meantime, we have had the good fortune to realise that we have joyful tidings to bring, to contribute not only to the faith of people, but also to the search for new ways in society. Good preparation and guidance renews the faith of people and puts them in a position to walk along these new ways.

In school catechesis here and there results are beginning to show. Renewal is not restricted to school catechesis alone. And frequently it is the catechists among the staff of a school who display the most feeling for, and experience in, educational renewal generally, especially when it comes to the principle of child-centred education. In the pastoral care of schools a start has also been made in training lay teachers to express their own life-convictions in their lessons. The development of this part-process of school catechesis can be considered the first phase in the renewal of religious education in general.

The second phase becomes the development of a part-process for family and parish. Primarily, this will have to be a form of adult catechesis. Yet we prefer not to use the term 'adult catechesis' because we are not directing ourselves exclusively to adults but to parents and children and to all concerned in the community of faith. Therefore we call it FAMILY CATECHESIS, PARISH CATECHESIS, COMMUNITY CATECHESIS.

'Family catechesis' is generally used to describe that form of adult catechesis to parents, which assists them in the religious education of their children.

When we want to express what we mean more accurately, we speak of a catechesis from within the parish *to* adults which

26

at the same time becomes a catechesis *from* these adults to their children: a family catechesis. Family catechesis is then, in the strictest sense everything that occurs at home between young and old in religious education.

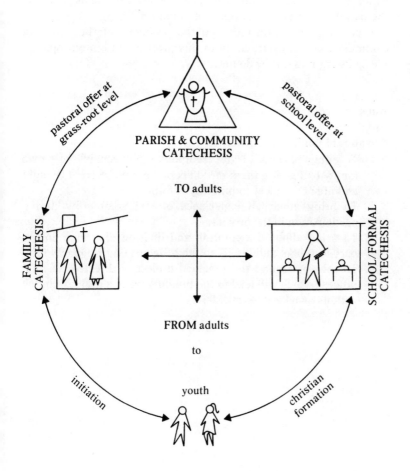

This family catechesis is definitely an adult affair in the sense that it is concerned with the questions and problems of adults themselves and the deepest questions and life-problems of all members of the household. It definitely does not aim at an infantile simplification of the mysteries of religion, as can happen when the school informs parents about what is being taught to their children. Some people call this, also, family catechesis, because the parents are asked to support at home what happens at school. The parents' own questions and the problems of the believing community do not figure at all in this process, and in our opinion it is quite right that they do not.

Aims

The aims of family catechesis are:
1. To equip parents to give religious education in their own family by leading them more deeply into the current thought and life of the local community of faith.
2. To bring about an experience of real community during participation in the project.
3. To bring about co-operation and division of labour among parish, school and family in the religious education of youth.
4. To set up, around the practical project, a directed pastoral process which will lead to the building up of a real lay church with its own local team of laity.

*Parents who hand over the
education of their children
to others are missing the
chance of a lifetime to
remain young and grow
up with them.*

4. EQUIPPING

The motto at the head of this section has come to sound like the
refrain of family catechesis. People who try to hand over the
religious education of their children, for example to the school or
the parish, eventually lose out. They forfeit the chance of a lifetime of remaining young with their children, of remaining up
to date and growing with them in their faith. They rule themselves
out. They bring to a halt their own development in relation to
their children. They stand still and their children go on. So the
parents fall behind. Sooner or later they find themselves in
trouble. Later on they will be unable to follow their children,
let alone lead them. Yet it is precisely the children who could
best help their parents to keep up to date.

All parents who hear this are inclined to endorse it at once.
They find it helpful to have their attention drawn to it. It opens
many eyes. Therefore our motto becomes a slogan. It gives many
parents the initial incentive to keep on listening, to find out what
the whole thing is about, to get the feel of it. Perhaps this time
it actually is what they have been waiting for, for so long . . . .
Strange, that even after this it still takes many parents a long time
to realise, or even accept that in the first place this is something
that concerns them. Yet the motto leaves little doubt about it. The
idea that parents, grown-up people, can still have something to
learn seems so strange to them that it is only after some months
that they come to this discovery: 'Yes, there is quite a lot in this
for me. We grown-ups don't know everything . . .'

Now care must always be taken that it does not turn into a
course of adult catechesis in the old style; that is the sort of
course customary in parishes where there is one speaker, somebody who knows all about it. He conducts the course and the

29

students sit at his feet as the ignorant who wish to be instructed. Of course, they do have group discussions, but no deep life-questions come from the participants because it is all about celibacy, ecumenism, the Third World. When the audience goes home it is not at all clear to each one what he can do with what was presented.

Traditional views of teaching and training are clearly the model here. These certainly give the director, the pastor, a clear view of his role and identity, but it puts adults back into the role of pupils. This recalls images of childhood which arouse disagreeable feelings that soon undermine their enthusiasm. This type of catechesis usually peters out . . . we see this happen over and over again.

It is not a course

Family catechesis is not a course run in the form of a series of parents' evenings. It is the EQUIPPING of parents through a number of parents' evenings, among other things. On the question of equipping, there are all sorts of opinions. A particularly persistent misconception is that it amounts to a kind of course for increasing knowledge or for acquiring a number of techniques in the religious or educational fields. Happily this is often a by-product. By *equipping*, we understand *a process of awareness and clarification whereby people learn once more to pose their own questions of faith. Furthermore they are assisted to express the religious dimension of their own lives and of their own actions, more particularly in so far as these affect the education of their children.* The real process of family catechesis only begins after the parents' evening is over. Family catechesis presupposes a very special type of approach, and is based on its own particular kind of motivation.

As far as the *method of approach* is concerned, the intention is that it should lead to interaction among all who take part, adults and children. All present determine, by their joint participation and contribution, the course the process of formation takes. For the director of formation, for the parents as well as for the pastor, this means their own on-going formation: they all learn continually from it. Everyone is thus more or less in the same position: equals in the same process. The novel approach, the surprise element, and the enrichment experienced are of prime importance for the motivation.

Towards a living church

The specific *motivation* of family catechesis consists in this, that we do not begin by laying down preconditions or presupposing a standard. The aim is not primarily to re-school the participants, but as we have already said, to *equip* them for a task with which they are already confronted and in which they have been engaged for some time already. It seeks to clarify a particular dimension of their lives — an awareness of the fact that everything they do and experience takes place in God. This religious dimension is always present, but perhaps they do not see it or they have lost sight of it. So we acknowledge that parents have their own role as adults and we show that we have full confidence in them as the first religious educators of their children. We take as our starting-point the conviction that every parent desires the best for his child (even if what he does is not always particularly successful in our eyes). With this respect for them and for their beliefs, we want to walk beside them, to find the way together towards an up-to-date religious education for their children. Family catechesis is always about things that are extremely practical and of immediate concern for parents. It is an offer made to them in which they recognise themselves in such a way that it immediately becomes part of them, a part which they in turn can pass on to their children, their family, their work, their surroundings.

So parents willingly come back time and again, hoping to learn more.

Indirect pastoral work

Adult catechesis done in this indirect way has, in our opinion, great advantages over a direct pastoral approach to these adults. People are better motivated if they discover that they mean something to others, especially to their own children. For this reason they are willing to learn a bit more. The indirect approach is also felt to be less threatening. For many people, to take part voluntarily in a religious course or bible group is a big step. They wonder what will be said behind their backs: 'Gosh, I never thought you were so religious'. 'Isn't he parading his religion a bit?' If you are doing it for your children, however, it is quite different.

Moreover, the indirect approach is less compelling, more inviting. It leaves more freedom. It leaves the options open, and people do not feel forced to accept the consequences of a particular insight in their own lives. That is not what they came for in the first place anyway. Each came for his child. What this might mean for himself is something he can always work out in his own time, if and when he gets round to it.

But when a person takes part in an adult catechesis aimed directly at him he can hardly avoid the consequences which arise. He has less freedom to consider privately whether this is for him or not. He is saddled with the consequences sooner, even if in his heart of hearts he does not feel ready for it yet.

PART II
CATECHESIS OF LIFE

*If something has no direct
message for their reality,
their problems, their lives,
people regard it as
superfluous, irrelevant,
accidental, in fact, as
superstition.*

Family catechesis is characterized by a number of aspects which generally come across as very positive.

* In the first place, family catechesis is a *realistic catechesis* because it starts from reality *and* remains within familiar experience, the familiar life-problems of people. The content of this catechesis is decided by these factors, and not by religious theories (p. 38).

* We also describe it as *meditative catechesis*. This is by contrast with an informative catechesis whose end is merely knowledge. Family catechesis concerns itself above all with questioning, searching and considering in a reflective way the things people already know and do, but in which they have not yet discovered the meditative depth (p. 43).

* Because this catechesis sets out to be religious education for young and old, we also call it *formation catechesis*. By this we definitely do not mean making the young fit the norms and church forms of adult believers. We want to help all concerned to discover the real values of life, especially the eternal values, in order that they may build their personal life of faith upon them (p. 48).

* Beside this, it is also a *relationship catechesis*. It is not exclusively concerned with the soul of the individual and his salvation, but with the experience of the religious community, with each member's place in it, with the many relationships, the mutual bonds, the covenant with God, and with communion in Christ (p. 54).

* Above all, family catechesis is an expressly *sacramental catechesis* of God's people on the way. The catechetical process takes the form of setting people on the road and then going along with them for the sanctification of all and for the salvation of society (p. 71).

Each of these characteristics has its own background. We shall go more deeply into this in the following pages.

Finally we shall summarise it in its entirety with the aid of a diagram: *catechesis and science* (p. 80).

5. REALISTIC CATECHESIS

In our youth, religious education was decidedly apologetic and dogmatic. Nowadays one comes across all kinds of approaches, depending very much on the performance of the teacher. One swears by the phenomenological approach to religion, another looks more to theology as a starting point, or exegesis, anthropology, sociology, or psychology. As long as it is called religious education we do not mind.

As soon as it is called catechesis, however, it becomes more of a problem. Firstly because sometimes the term catechesis is used to describe a course, for example in dogma, scripture, or a related human science. Secondly, and even more so, because this would suggest that catechesis is really a scientific affair and that the giving of catechesis must be reserved for specialists in one or other of the religious sciences.

You throw ordinary people into a state of panic if you ask them to give catechesis to children in the parish. In many primary schools teachers do not feel equipped to give catechesis either. This goes to show that there has been a considerable narrowing of the concept of catechesis.

This is all the more serious because in this way a large group of ordinary believers, the layfolk, are being excluded from an activity for which they have a particular innate responsibility, one which simply cannot be farmed out or delegated to specialists. What are we doing about all the ordinary parents, and the religious education they should be giving their children? What are the implications for the great majority of the teachers in our catholic schools if ordinary people aren't considered able to give catechesis properly? It creates enormous confusion if, at the same time, parents and teachers are told that they are primarily 'responsible' for the religious education of children, at home or at school. In the case of family catechesis we draw in ordinary parishioners. So we must pose the question: are we, or are we not, serious when we say that they are primarily responsible for the religious education of their children?

By education in the faith we surely don't mean an influence that only takes place unconsciously, unnoticed and unspoken? That is certainly not the intention of family catechesis. An education that doesn't regularly bring up for discussion the subject of its own motives and criteria is not education, it is indoctrination. Catechesis, in the sense of proclaiming, relating or putting across 'the good news' has been, from the earliest times, the way of introducing people to, and educating them in, the faith. In essence, by catechesis everyone means — even now — the giving of religious education in this sense. But then catechesis cannot be primarily a scientific affair. Education in the faith operates on quite a different level to that of a scientific dissertation. Religious education requires witness rather than exposition of the facts of faith. The why of what you believe is difficult to demonstrate.

The task of every believer

Family catechesis consciously opts for the catechesis of everyday life: for a definite education in faith and witness of faith which is the task of every ordinary Christian. 'By virtue of her calling', said the Second Vatican Council, 'the church carries out her pastoral task through all her members, each in his own way' (Laity Decree, 2). 'All are called by the Lord himself to this apostolate by their baptism and confirmation, especially in the places and circumstances where it is only through them that the community of faith can be the salt of the earth' (Constitution on the church, 33). It is not only the duty but also the right of everyone who has been baptised and confirmed (Laity Decree, 3 and 25). Therefore it must lie within the capabilities of every believer.

It is high time that we give catechesis back to those primarily responsible, and regard it once more as something which lies within the reach of every Christian, not just of the cleric or of the subject-teacher. Those who hold positions of leadership in the church should bear in mind that they do not have a monopoly when it comes to catechesis. That right and duty are the common possession of all the faithful; the laity has a unique role. The clergy must know how to open the way for them and guide them along it (cf Laity Decree, 25).

This is not something new, invented in Amsterdam or the Netherlands. In 1971, the French catechist Bournique was speaking from experience when he said, at the International Catechetical Conference in Rome: 'It is in complete accordance with the theological vision of the active role of the people of God, that as many as possible of the faithful should be involved in catechesis. This was emphasised in Vatican II. In many places it has in fact proved possible to involve parents in the catechesis of children and adolescents. The catechesis of the adults themselves, however, only becomes alive and effective when adults realise their mutual responsibility for each other's formation. It is of the utmost importance that every diocese should have a team of highly qualified professional catechists but they must try, as far as possible, to engage all the faithful in catechetical work. The professional can then give the necessary support and can provide the catechetical material.'*

Is it still acceptable?

We are probably raising a number of questions for those people who think this is all very well, but who doubt if such things can be permitted these days. What sort of catechesis is it? What is it worth? Has it any content? What kind of foundation does it have?

From the first days of Christendom, catechesis has meant the enthusiastic proclamation of what has happened in our world and in our own lives, 'concerning Jesus of Nazareth, who was a prophet mighty in deed and word, before God and all the people' (Luke 24: 19).

In this connection, the bible states clearly that deeds come before words. That is important. Action precedes proclamation in the life of Jesus; and so it does in everyone's life. There must be a deed before there can be a living word, then one has the right to speak. Otherwise it is just an empty word transmitted to others. In the Acts of the Apostles we find particularly good examples

*Quoted in *Verbum* 39, 1972/1.

of this: plain, clearly set out statements, which were alive and concrete and which told with enthusiasm the things that the first Christians had experienced and lived and consequently could speak about. With regard to the content of this catechesis we should like to state that it is 'the clarification of everyday reality stemming from salvific faith in the God of Jesus Christ'.* By this we do not only mean the 'what' — the verbal transmission. Catechesis is a far broader occurrence within the context of human encounter. The report on the evangelisation of Europe states: 'We aren't short of words which have to be passed on to people, but what we are short of is credible people who can pass on the word.'† In Acts we read of the message being enthusiastically proclaimed and joyfully transmitted. We have experienced something similar among people who are involved in family catechesis.

What happens here catechetically, is certainly determined by what is said, the *content*, but this is dependent on the *attitude* of the person who speaks: that is the extent to which he speaks from experience, the extent to which he lives up to the ideal personally and to the quality of the *relationships* in which all this is proclaimed. If, in the relationships between catechist and catechised, a contradiction is experienced; if the opposite of what is being preached in such beautiful words is practised, the untruthfulness evokes rejection and aggression rather than faith.

The full content of this catechesis is fourfold: the people themselves as they live and believe; their actions and omissions within mutual relationships; the credibility of this process; and finally the proclamation which flows from this.

Therefore, we speak of a 'realistic catechesis', or of a 'catechesis of life'. In this catechesis, we are not concerned primarily with matters of faith outside ourselves, but rather with the believing dimension of our own faith in the realities of everyday life. By 'realistic' we mean that the content of this catechesis cannot be traced back to any scientific discipline whatsoever, but is rooted in life itself, of which faith is one dimension. This faith is always present in one way or another. It is one of the factors determining what we do and say and, as such, it can be discussed.

The question immediately arises as to how one should visualise

---

*J. Bulckens, in *Verbum* 40, 1973/5.
†Synod of Bishops, 1974.

this catechesis in practice if it appears to have little or no content. It is difficult to understand why people suddenly jump to the conclusion that it can't be about anything important or that we are dealing with next to nothing, because we are not discussing some 'scientific' subject. No one could maintain that the preaching of St Paul was about nothing or that he taught the people nothing. Yet he says quite emphatically in his first letter to the Corinthians: 'When I came to you, I did not come proclaiming to you the testimony of God in lofty words or wisdom. For I decided to know nothing among you except Jesus Christ and him crucified. And I was with you in weakness and in much fear and trembling; and my speech and my message were not in plausible words of wisdom, but in demonstration of the Spirit and of power, that your faith might not rest in the wisdom of men but in the power of God' (1 Cor 2:1-5).

We really have in mind a catechesis such as Jesus himself gave to the ordinary people of the time: one that could be understood by everyone, and was taken directly from life; the Kingdom of Heaven is like a grain of wheat, a lost coin, a mustard seed, workers in the vineyard, a man on the road, all everyday things. Behind all these things of everyday life the mystery is hidden: the Kingdom of Heaven is among you, but at the same time, it still has to come, it still has to be fulfilled. A great many people do not see this, do not make it come true. This catechesis sees good news in all the small and great things of every day, and finds glad tidings in the small happenings of every moment.

The content of this catechesis is the little story of every believer, the story of his own struggle but also the story of the source from which he obtains the strength to carry on and to continue believing and hoping. This familiar story is the thread of joy and sorrow which is woven into the whole of salvation history as we piece it together day after day. The history of salvation is not just made up of the stories of the few great ones but of the stories of all people together, of the people of God on their way.

*One can regard every
reality in two ways: as a
fact and as a mystery.*

6. MEDITATIVE CATECHESIS

These days all of us, both adults and children, have an enormous amount to digest, absorb and assimilate. And more is added every day. From all sides new things continually assail us. We are constantly drawn outwards, away from our inward being, away from the depth of things. Everything is absorbed superficially and hurriedly. But in this way we come into contact with only one side of things: the superficial side, the outside. However, one can look at every reality in two ways: as a fact and as a mystery.

Factual knowledge, however scientifically exact and precise, is only concerned with one side of human knowing. Such knowledge is therefore one-sided if it is not complemented by deeper knowledge: by the contemplative, intuitive, meditative knowing through which one sees depth, context, spiritual power, human life values, and eternal values, and eventually God Himself.

When the deep well of meditative knowing is permanently lacking, a man's thinking dries up. It becomes harsh and hard as rock. Indeed we see this happening more and more around us daily, in an inflexible business world in which we are all yearning for a little more humanity.

We hardly realise how important water is in our daily life. As long as it is present in sufficient quantities and keeps everything moist then all nature is healthy, green and alive. Only when everything around us dries up and dies, when all becomes a barren desert, then we suddenly realise what it is we are missing: water.

On a spiritual level something similar is happening at present in our society. If the life-giving dew of God's Spirit does not fall upon society and drench it, life becomes arid, stony, meaningless and unlivable. Only a meditative meeting with God in all human experiences can give freshness and meaning to our lives, our relationships and our daily events. Meditative knowledge is not something we must just drag in, as an appendix, along with the factual knowledge that we must absorb. It is not something that is added. And it is certainly not something accidental. It is a dimension of life itself with which we are occupied daily — the dimension of faith.

Meditative knowledge calls to life what is already present, slumbering in our depths. It fills us with wonder and joy to discover the values which are hidden beneath surface realities.

Most people regard the actualities of their daily life as things to be taken for granted: air, food, work, recognition by others, people who care. Fish live in water and don't know it. Animals and people live in air and don't stop to think about it. We live in God and are not even aware of it. That is exactly how self-evident the religious dimension, that divine milieu, is, and just how indispensable it is. As long as all these riches of life are taken for granted, or demanded as a right, they arouse no wonder or gratitude. Neither do they offer any encouragement to explore them more deeply.

However, all the things we take for granted are regularly disrupted by life itself. Usually this happens in an extremely painful way: through an illness, a death, an accident. We are suddenly shocked by the realisation that many things which we never really appreciated because we always took them for granted, are disappearing. Now we are confronted with a strange void and the reaction is usually confusion, fright, opposition, sorrow that we did not appreciate them before and that we were so careless about them when everything was going well.

The things we take for granted can also be disrupted in a happy way. This is less painful, particularly formative and enriching. With meditative catechesis we invite young and old to take a deeper look at their own lives. We help them to develop an insight into the reasons why everything runs smoothly and as a matter of course: why we have it so good now; the reasons behind it all; what is involved. In the first place this arouses in us a sense of wonder at how many people co-operate harmoniously and are ready to serve one another, and how miraculously everything in nature and in our own lives is interrelated and linked. And that in turn leads to gratitude, satisfaction, openness, happiness, and a *joie de vivre* which nowadays is often hard to find.

It is this meditative attitude which once more turns a person into a seeker, a thinking person, one who discovers rich human values behind all the forms and norms of our society. It helps a believer discover once again God's action in the ordinary things of every day.*

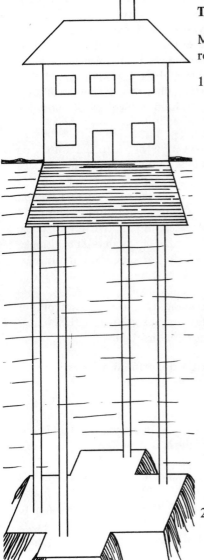

Three phases

Meditative catechesis considers reality in three phases:

1. We start out from the reality in which we are involved daily; the usual run of affairs, *human behaviour*, and the common life of every day. As long as everything goes well, then life runs smoothly and matter-of-factly and reality is so ordinary that nobody worries about what is behind it all. Only when something goes wrong does it strike us. But when we have a situation in which things go wrong, it then becomes evident that adults and children alike have never stopped to think about the wonderful order which lies hidden behind all things, even on the human level. They only see the outside: a house, a family, parents, children. But what is a house without foundations, or a family without communication? What are parents without love, or children without gratitude and joy?

2. Therefore we seek together that which lies beneath our common humanity. We search for the fundamentally human,

*Marcel van Caster, in *Tijdschrift voor catechese*, 4(1974) 4, 241-52.

the reason, the explanation, the deeper meaning, the bonds and the cohesion that exist between people and their behaviour. In short, we are seeking the human values which are hidden beneath all ordinary things and which are so well covered by all the *norms*, customs and usages that everything runs smoothly and automatically as a result. So we discover that because of good foundations and steel support the house stands firmly, because of the co-operation of parents and children there is sound family life. Even if we do not delve any further than this deeper level then the searching together at a purely human level gives much joy and enrichment.

3. Catechetical questioning, however, is not satisfied with, and does not stop at, the human significance but questions and probes further into the deepest sense and meaning of everything. At this point it really becomes a reflection on what we see around us, and what we experience and discover within ourselves, and a meditation on the meaning of these things. We try to make people open themselves gradually to these wonders and to make them sensitive to *eternal values*, to the deepest significance which, for a believer, lies beneath all human norms and forms and beneath all the actions of every individual.

It does not rest until it has found the true ground of our existence and of all reality, and its deepest significance. Ultimately it is a seeking for God, here and now, in this reality.

For example: We can say that good communication exists in a family because its members are in communion in Christ; because parents and children are conscious of the fact that they have been entrusted to each other by God. No matter how excellent the quality of the foundations, if it is stuck in marshy ground and does not rest on rock, it will not support the house for long. In this sense we understand what Matthew wrote (7:24 ff): A man was so foolish as to build his house upon sand; and the rains fell, and the floods came, and the winds blew, and beat against the house and it collapsed completely. Another man was wise enough to build on rock and the rain fell and floods came and the winds blew and beat against that house but it remained standing because it had been founded on rock.

In his book *Meer dan het gewoone*, Boerwinkel says: the foundation by which the house is kept standing is not a particular doctrine, nor a creed of faith, not even the bible (however holy it may be). The foundation, according to Jesus himself, is doing what he taught in the Sermon on the Mount, that is, doing justice, doing the will of the Father (Mt. 7:21-22). This catechesis is definitely not designed to provide knowledge about all kinds of facts related to a doctrine, a creed, a church denomination. It is designed to encourage meditative knowledge, in-depth knowledge of our own interior motivations; an understanding of how we can live and act in answer to the invitation God gives us every moment of our lives.

This catechesis is decidedly not aiming at providing factual knowledge of our religion, but meditative knowledge, knowledge in depth of the life-values which are ordinarily present. The method which uses experience-data only as an opening gambit and moves immediately to a treatment of comparable religious data does not fit into this scheme. The following is an example of that kind of approach: the catechist focusses people's attention on something that they consider important, but finding himself unable to use the situation effectively he falls back on 'religious data' or a story which has little or no bearing on the catechesis. The catechist for instance begins like this: 'Did you hear the parliamentary debate on the radio on Wednesday? Well, that's the way it was when Moses was in the desert!' By moving straight into the subject of Moses and dwelling on that, nobody becomes any the wiser about the present debate, here and now.

Everything that we present which has no direct message for people's reality, their problems, and their lives they will look upon as superfluous, irrelevant, accidental, in fact, as superstition. That is the fate of much informative catechesis which is mainly concerned with knowledge. Our aim is to be thoughtfully and reflectively concerned with all that people do, know and experience daily, in order to give it meditative depth.

*By what right does any
person presume that he
may or must interfere with
the conduct of another
person?*

7. FORMATION CATECHESIS

That catechesis is 'religious education' seems obvious to us.
But let us examine just how obvious it is. Education is more than
mere instruction. It is directed towards influencing people's
behaviour. Religious education is directed towards giving people,
young and old, such formation as will lead them to behave as
believers. We are even blessed with a sacrament related to this:
confirmation.

Many people have problems with this notion of education. 'Is
it permissible to exert such an influence on anybody? Or is it
permissible only up to ten or twelve years old?' In our opinion,
the real question underlying these is: 'By what right does any
person presume that he may or must interfere with the conduct
of another, especially in a matter of such fundamental importance?
May a community, a people, a church body, authorise him to do
so? What power or right of decision does such a body presume to
have over the liberty and consciences of its people and children?
By what authority does it act?'

Until recently it was usually claimed that this authority came
from God. But, fortunately, great doubts have arisen as to whether
any one person or even a group can abrogate to themselves
the authority to prescribe for another precisely how God intends
that he should behave. On what privileged relationship with God
is this founded?

We now realise that one person cannot prescribe at random
what another should follow blindly. Everyone has his own conscience. Only if he cannot manage by himself and only if he
accepts the intervention of another as a service or a favour, would
such an intervention be justifiable.

This brings us straight to the heart of the problem of education in general, and to the heart of the problem of religious education in particular. The saying of Jesus that He did not come to rule or to compel, but to serve and to assist, is, in our opinion, of fundamental importance in this area of education. It indicates precisely what should be the place and attitude of the catechist. It is absolutely clear that catechesis should never be experienced as coercive or compulsive.

It should be experienced as an education which serves, as good news, as something which people appreciate because it is so valuable.

Our values, norms and behaviour

We can draw a clear distinction between *behaviour norms* and *values*. This distinction has come to permeate and be relevant to each aspect of Family Catechesis — realistic, meditative, formative, relationship and sacramental. We will now try to clarify exactly what we do and do not mean by the terms *behaviour norms* and *values*.

The distinction between *norms* and *values* is of the utmost importance because these two terms are often interchanged. We feel that many misunderstandings and mistakes made in introducing changes, many complaints, accusations and reproaches made about changes in church and society are the consequences of a misunderstanding of what is essential and what is accidental. We must understand what are real values and what are the norms and expressions of them.

When we say that many religious forms and aspects are manmade and therefore only secondary and accidental, many people get up in arms because they feel that we are tampering with the holiest 'values'. Therefore we shall try to clarify our good intentions (see also Table I, p. 80, particularly column IV.)

As human beings, we accept a large number of *values*, for example to live and let live, to love and be loved, to be happy, to be healthy, to belong and to mean something to others, to be known, appreciated and trusted, to be loyal, to feel safe and cared for, to live in peace, to be free, to be given room for growth ... All these are values which cannot be bought, which we do not have entirely in our own control, which have been bestowed on us

49

in some way or another, but which cause us to believe in life and in other people, in short, values which make life worth living.

These values determine our behaviour, our actions, how we present ourselves to others, how we treat them, what we strive after. To prevent a number of values being destroyed, we make agreements to accommodate each other and we regulate things in such a way that we take each others' interests into account.

It is rather striking that, among all peoples and cultures, this process has given rise to the same phenomenon, viz. the development of *norms*.

This must, therefore, be a fundamentally human phenomenon. In so far as a specific group attaches importance to some of these agreed practices, it tends to turn them into traditions and customs. These become rules and conventions and eventually laws and norms. So each nation grows towards a culture-pattern of its own and develops its own distinct concepts of what is good, beautiful, rich and noble. We want to emphasise that here we are dealing with purely human arrangements which were largely determined by circumstances. But perhaps they are also attempts to gain some control over the intangible elements present in these fundamentally human values.

They are not the only possible or only correct norms and forms, however holy they may be for certain groups or people. Anything that is a norm, an accepted form, any such expression, even in religion, is man-made, and is bound to time and space. It is always secondary to the values to which it tries to give shape.

It may seem strange that the system of norms of a certain group of people carries so much weight that in the long run a person's behaviour is determined not by what he deems important and valuable, but by what the laws and norms prescribe. We see this happening in primitive tribes, and in modern nations and groups (just think of the world of fashion!). It also happens in religion.

From this it is clear that a person's behaviour may be dependent either on values, or on norms, and the two are not the same thing. For, although the norms grew out of certain values at a particular time, this does not mean that these same norms are the best expression of these values, or still serve these values, today. The norms have begun to live a life of their own. They are tangible. People who do not have much depth attach more importance to the norms than to the real values. They begin to call the norms themselves 'values' and eventually to glorify them as the highest values of all. And this gives rise to great confusion.

All this has important consequences for education which aims at influencing behaviour. Education takes place either according to norms or according to values. Two totally different educational models have developed as a consequence:

1. the adaptation model (adapting the person to the group) and

2. the development model (developing the person).

The adaptation model

The adaptation model is by far the most common. Especially in the early years of childhood one can hardly avoid using it. By the very language parents speak, they lead their children almost without knowing it into their own cultural pattern and teach them the customs and norms which are peculiar to their nation. They teach them to eat, sit, walk and talk 'nicely'. And this results in a particular type of behaviour. Like father, like son.

For all practical purposes, the adaptation model has come to be regarded as the only correct one. To this day it is the most natural way, people say. In actual fact it is not natural, but is built on human constructions and regulations with all their human limitations and shortcomings. Yet they are turned into absolutes and maintained with authority: 'The norms and regulations are clear!' But on what grounds are these regulations based? 'Orders are orders!' 'All you have to do is to regulate your conduct accordingly.' 'But by what right are these orders given?' 'It is not open to discussion!' 'There must be law and order'.

What the values of certain norms may be is not always clear. But even here nobody dares to question them. 'That's the way it has always been, and therefore it is good.'

The *norms are given priority* and education becomes an impersonal formal process. The educator with his personality and his own personal life does not enter into the process. As long as he ensures that the norms are put across to his pupils and that their behaviour complies with these, then he has done his duty. This is admittedly a caricature, but in fact, that is how this education-model has often operated and perhaps still does!

The development model

The development model places the person at the centre, and concerns itself with his health, his growth, his happiness, the full development of each individual's personality in his association with the other. Everyone can and should be involved in this process all his life. This type of education is not a formal, impersonal exercise in which the educator can test his pupils one by one against the norms, while he as an individual merely monitors it from the outside.

It is a human process of interaction in which, time and again, the significance and the value of each person's behaviour in relation to others is brought into play. It is an education process in which all the educators are involved. Old and young bring each other up, and become truly human through each other in the events of life, the happenings of every day. It is a collective process of growth, an ongoing education.

In this educational model human concerns take precedence over all impersonal norms and demands. *Behaviour* and *values* are given priority and norms are of *secondary* importance, which is what they essentially are: aids for the purpose of regulating human interaction. People and their relationships, their behaviour in respect of each other, and the living out of actual life-values between them are indeed living realities. These should never be suppressed by the dead letter of the norm and the law. On the other hand it is true that a number of accepted norms or customs can render good service for a long time so that every action or mutual arrangement does not have to be thought out, debated and worked out from zero. But they should be immediately subject to review when they cease to be clear. This will ensure that attention remains focussed on life values.

Formation catechesis is a type of religious education within the development model. It is therefore not a catechesis about faith, doctrine or a number of truths as if it were concerned with impersonal objective facts which one person can teach another. It is the sort of education which puts the life and conduct of all who are involved in it under scrutiny. It probes, on a faith level, its deeper sense and value, in order to be able to live a better life as a believer.* It is in line with the Christian notion of human

*Joseph Colomb, 'A modern approach to catechesis in the Church', *Concilium* (English edition) 1970-3, pp. 22-3.

development as expressed in *Populorum Progressio* 14: 'What counts for us Christians is the human being, every human being, every group of human beings, the whole human community.'

It is a service stemming from the deepest human values, from religious values in fact. It leads to the development and growth of every believer, of the whole believing community, and of the whole of human society, a service offered for 'the development of the nations.'

8. RELATIONSHIP CATECHESIS

When we asked ourselves by what right a group or nation could impose laws or norms we remarked in passing that, until recently, people usually claimed that the authority to do so came from God. We now want to examine this phenomenon more deeply, because it is not something which merely happened now and then. We see that from the earliest times, among all nations and tribes, this has been the case, so much so that religion and culture, the sacred and the profane, formed one organic whole, and, in fact, coincided.

In our day this phenomenon is explained as follows: wise and intelligent people designed a number of sound customs, forms and norms which regulated relationships in the group. In order to give these rules sufficient authority, so that everyone would keep them, they did not disclose that they had thought them up themselves, but they invented (for the ordinary mass of people) a higher power which had inspired the laws or had handed them over personally. Consequently these laws which regulate the relationships between people differ from nation to nation. They may be attributed either to priests, elders, kings, priest-kings or other men of God. The transgressing or breaking of the divine laws was regarded as an insult to God himself, a serious sin against divine right, and therefore against good order in society, of which these men of God were custodians. Sooner or later it called down God's anger on the evildoers.

For a phenomenon which is so characteristic of mankind and its religions, the explanation seems far too superficial. Right up to the beginning of the century this was still the accepted theory. Such a phenomenon, however, could not occur everywhere merely by chance. When patterns appear persistently and independently, then we can suspect that they reveal an underlying reality based on the experience of some deeper foundation, some deeper value.

Just as we ourselves experience life as believers, we presume that our forefathers, in appealing to the authority of God, were making known that as far as they could see, all our happy associations with each other, our good relationships, everything which we experience as good in our existence, are based on still deeper 'eternal' values. They were aware, just as we are, that 'I' does not explain 'myself' nor am I sufficient unto myself.

The I — YOU, I-and-the-others relationship, is not a complete explanation either. From this comes a conviction that we stand together within the larger context of the mystery of our existence, and that there is a definite relationship between us human beings and that mystery. This in turn led to the belief that there is a Third Party besides me and the others in this covenant: God.

'The tragedy of this generation is that men have completely lost this relationship with God so that they now imagine that relationships between people are the most sacred charge of life' says Kierkegaard. That is what it often looks like. Yet we think we have gone beyond this. We still want to be free of a God who gives authority to human laws and norms. But once again there is a longing for contact with the deepest mystery, the eternal values, the surest ground of our human existence.

In the previous chapter we tried to distinguish the human values (that is being healthy and belonging, loving and being loved, being trusted and being faithful, feeling free and secure, living in peace) from the norms and rules which have gradually arisen to guarantee these values. We established that we had no firm hold on these values, that we could not buy them, because they were not of our own making. Good relationships with others contribute to these values, but the others have no more control over them than we do.

In one way or another they are given to us. In spite of all our efforts, we are quite helpless in a number of situations. Life is full of surprises! The development of science has made little real difference in this respect.

This experience, that we exist together within a greater context, that we are taken up in one great mystery, that there is a relation between us and that mystery, would seem to be the basic experience from which religions have originated.

Not only the wonderful order, the perfect life process, but also the surprise happening — which outsiders dismiss as 'coincidence' — are understood by the initiated as clear signs and revelations of a higher reality which concerns itself with them.

'Coincidence' is an inadequate explanation for certain happenings. It is even less adequate, as an explanation of the wonders of creation, than the belief in a higher reality that is involved with creation and also with us: the belief in an intelligent reality which we can get to know through his great works and constant activity. People have tried with words, gestures and actions to give expression to these experiences, and tried to make contact with the mysterious reality. Hence the many philosophies of life, which have their own unique vision of the world, and the numerous religious cultural patterns, religions and denominations which in turn give concrete shape to the philosophies through particular forms and norms, laws and prescriptions, rites and phenomena. Through these, people have tried to make tangible and communicable that which can never be completely captured in words and images.

In gesture and movement it became possible for all the initiated to experience the mystery together. If you know the stories behind the gestures and you join in, then it can happen, then the experience can be yours, the spark, the flame, the enthusiasm can take hold of you: you realise that there is more here than what can be seen or heard or said, or done.

Religious circle experience

In our secularised world the religious circle experience has to a large extent been lost — and to some degree this is even true of our church. Yet group experience persists in the secularised world and it seems that even there an authentic yearning for the fundamental religious experience is perceived. What happens in a crowded stadium, or at a pop festival or happening is regarded by some as a remnant of religion or even as a new expression of it. The numbers are somewhat larger, but is such a surging crowd really so very different from the religious ring dances of primitive people in the forests, or a final campfire at the end of a wonderful holiday camp? Like-minded people sit next to each other and there in the middle of the circle 'it' happens; there the fire burns, there the ball bounces, there the music sounds, but at the same time much more happens than what is merely seen or heard.

Each one feels himself caught up in the atmosphere, a feeling of belonging to each other. Mysterious powers are aroused.

Could not these events be a remote substitute for what takes place at a genuine religious happening? There we are with a group of people. We feel that we belong together. We have a sense of the mystery in our midst which brings us together. We perceive something which we find valuable, something we believe in, which continues to draw us together, which binds and inspires us communally, which is of a totally different order from that in a stadium or pop festival. Is this a delusion? That is what people often accuse us of. Is it wishful thinking, is there nothing really happening?

As Christians we believe that we come together around the unfathomable depths of the divine mystery in our midst, the mystery in which we are caught up and in which we feel bound to each other. We are aware that this is the ground of our existence, of our life and happiness, but also that it transcends all our powers of understanding and imagination. Therefore we do not try to make this mystery, God, tangible through substitutes like camp-fires, football, music festivals or such like.

But should we? As human beings, are we not bound with the spiritual reality tangible to our experiences? Doesn't this happen in all great events and especially in the experiences of the fundamental mystery of our existence? We all know that being together in a group of like-minded people, being happy, singing, dancing together, gives us the experience of something which is more than the sum of me + the others. Afterwards we describe it as a wonderful atmosphere, as an extraordinarily pleasant day. That's the best we can do to explain it to someone who was not there. Being 'present' is an essential condition of the experience.

But the experience of that mysterious 'something extra' for which we have no words, which so overwhelms us as a feeling of happiness, the experience of 'being taken up into a larger whole', is not lasting. It is always momentary, fleeting.

Yet we dearly want to hold on to it. We want to capture it. Nowadays we take photographs which we can use to illustrate our stories to describe how marvellous it all was. Yet we know that the photos and stories mean something only to the people who shared the experience. They mean little or nothing to outsiders. They leave them untouched.

So the photos and stories cannot be judged 'objectively'. The

1. COMMUNITY

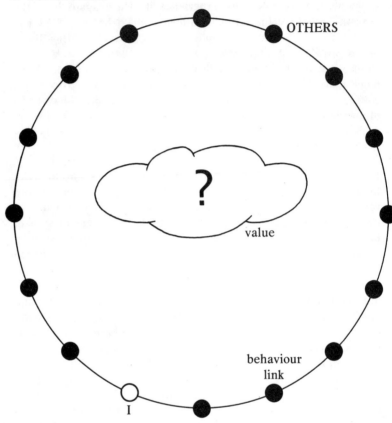

experience of that mysterious 'something extra' is definitely part of it. That 'something extra' is really what it is all about. It is the 'value' that was experienced, and of which the photos and stories are the expression. This is a clear example of a value-experience and its expression, and the continual tension which exists between the two. What is a worthless photo to one person may have, for another, the 'extra' value of an unforgettable experience.

The tensions between valuable signs and stories and empty, worthless, valueless forms, prescriptions and rites can be found in the religions of every age.

Many people, young and old, use the word 'worthless' to

indicate how they feel about everything to do with church and religion. That is how they experience it. Here again it is the tension between value-norms and forms and behaviour, how you experience it, where you stand in relation to it, on the inside or the outside.

We want to try to sketch, in broad outline, how various religions have struggled with this tension, to indicate the shifts which constantly occur between this living experience and the setting up of norms and forms as absolutes; the shift from living experience to dead regulations, and through this, the shift from community to society.

1. *Community*

In our opinion the most characteristic symbol of a community is a circle. That is why we choose the circle as the basic pattern for all our further considerations. A real circle is not simply any form of being together, loosely connected, with every man for himself, like a group of curious people gathered round a vendor at the market or an acrobat at the circus.

In a real circle all those present are participants. There is a hand-in-hand feeling between I and the others, a new, mutual bond, which is often tangible and which is expressed in the behaviour of the group as a whole: in their singing and dancing, sitting, walking, kneeling, moving, rejoicing, mourning.

The first requirement for community is being present. He who is not present cannot really talk about it.

Without this direct physical involvement there is no bond with the others. The second requirement for community is the collective motive, the collective value around which people gather, the common centre through which one becomes involved with others. Someone who does not become involved does not experience anything. For that person the whole affair is worthless. (Someone who does not like football is bored and irritated in a stadium.)

We would imagine that the religious gathering of the earliest tribes in the jungle were like this: that they were circle-experiences of all the members of the group, in which the adults were initiated and into which the children were gradually introduced. The characteristics of these communities were a strong living bond with each other and a direct experience of a mystery in their midst; often an ecstatic experience.

2. *Group*

Presumably, after the first ecstatic experience, the desire must have been awakened in people to preserve something of it, to capture something of it, to set up a memorial.

They sought out the place where they had experienced the ecstasy, and if the experience was repeated the place became a special one, a 'holy' place. (Doesn't everyone treasure some well-loved place from his past, a place he loves to go back to?) To mark this place accurately, a sign was put up, a stone or a statue erected. At subsequent gatherings the gestures and movements were recalled. 'Do you remember when we did such-and-such and then that feeling came over us?' These were familiar, ordinary human attempts designed to capture something of the inexpressible and unforgettable happenings that vanish so quickly in time. Many religious practices originated and developed in this way.

But people did not only have happy experiences. They were also prey to anxiety and pain, fear and sorrow, deadly agony and despair. Gradually men began to surmise that there were higher powers behind all this, a spiritual world which was favourably or unfavourably disposed towards people. These were not mere figments of their imagination, but they were thought-images attempting to explain the real experiences which transcended the individual and the group as a whole, to which they felt related and on which they depended.

Just as people succeeded in recalling happy experiences (the good spirits) so they also tried to wrestle with the threatening powers (the evil spirits). This was probably an attempt to gain through gestures and words some measure of control over the incomprehensible mystery of suffering which overcame them. Then they would not feel completely helpless or at the mercy of fate, but could perhaps do something about it themselves.

It is a fact that, from the earliest times, men have made attempts to capture these mysterious experiences of their relations with higher powers and to make them visible and tangible through movements, formulas, objects and places. There is nothing strange or senseless in this as a means to an end. We still have the need to grasp the spiritual and express it in the material. We ourselves are living examples of this.

When it becomes dangerous, however, is when the correct outlook on such a shape or form gets lost, when people no longer know the mystery that lies behind this form or that image. Then the means become an end in themselves, they become holy, sacred things in themselves, divine rules. That seems to be a common human experience. Time and again the higher powers were localised at specific holy places and their purposes became completely identified with the holy things and rituals.

Now what does it mean for a community when this kind of shift takes place from the living experience of values to the absolutising of the rules and the forms? It means that such a community will fall prey to 'religious materialism'. The material forms, the means, the things become holier than the spiritual, the mystery, the people and their experiences. The experience of God is increasingly controlled by 'divine' laws and rules which determine the behaviour of the people in the group down to the minutest details. The 'divine' is shifted from the value to the norm, from the essential interior to the accidental exterior, from the living experience to the dead system, from the continually new living encounter with God now to the lifeless tradition of the past.

So it is not difficult to see how the social, the economic, the moral, and the religious aspects of life flowed into each other to form one sacred unit of culture and religion.

It is reasonable to assume that the many different outward forms of religion arose in this way. People often understood the word 'religion' itself as a 'binding' element composed of those things which regulate and express the relationship between specific people, and between them and the supernatural.

It is important to keep in mind that the rules and norms of those relationships, the 'religious forms', are a very different thing from the religious happenings which underlie them: very different from 'the religious encounter' in which all feel themselves to be mutually united, and the religious values which are its foundation. These often become progressively obscure.

Because of this shift, the solidarity and unity that characterised the group alters. In an organisation or institute, the living bond which existed between 'I' and the others, and the direct relationship between all together and the mystery, can diminish or altogether disappear.

Mutual bonds are replaced by the objective bond of the norms and rules. Belonging is no longer so dependent on being present and participating. As long as you are a member, you belong. You have your rights and duties. You become a member by being told

2. GROUP

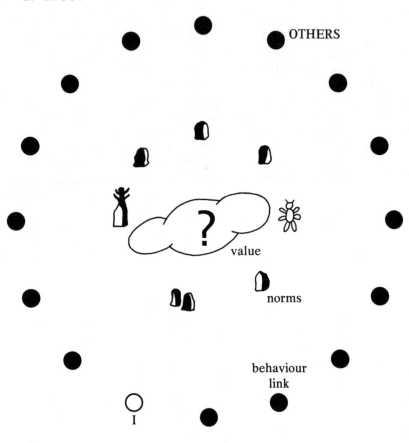

about the rules and by accepting them. By distinguishing yourself in keeping the rules you can become a more exemplary member.

The mutual relationships become loosely connected, accidental and based on the rules. Each person stands alone and is sufficient unto himself, as long as he takes care to keep the rules. What a neighbour does is his own business. The relationship to the value because of which he belongs to the group is indirect, through the means. This is the familiar model of every association, club or society, often even of religious congregations. A person is not so much a member because of the others who belong but because of the values and the importance that he finds in it for himself, and for which he takes a number of obligations upon himself.

3. *Nation*

We cannot say that the bonds of unity between those who belonged to the same religion became as totally depersonalised as we have just described. This was because other kinds of ties played a role as well: blood ties. These kept the people in the outer circle bound to each other as a tribe and as a nation. Religion was usually experienced as tribal or national. Each nation had its own religion. A good example of this is the Jewish people.

There is another reason for us to be particularly grateful to the Jews. It was among the Jewish people, surrounded by all kinds of ideas and opinions about a vast number of higher powers, that the conviction gradually grew that there is only One Other, Jahweh, the one true God of all people, races, tribes and tongues. This is faith and cannot be proved. Through their acceptance of Jahweh's covenant they opened up the possibility of a world faith, of a religion that could transcend the boundaries and bonds of a nation.

And yet, Judaism also went the way we sketched in Section 2. It continually burned its fingers in attempts to make the invisible visible, to comprehend the incomprehensible, prove the unprovable . . . at least for the benefit of the insiders.

The Hebrews condemned and rejected gold, bronze and stone idols. Quite soon, however, they honoured the stone tables as the laws of God and added to these a large number of holy things. We may read one striking example of this whole process in Joshua chapter 24. Joshua called all the tribes together and put before them once more all that Jahweh had done for them since the exodus from Egypt, how he had saved them and given them a new country. Finally he set before them the choice: 'Whom do you want to serve: the living God who has done and continues to do everything for you, or the dead idols of other nations?' The people answered: 'We would not dream of deserting Jahweh and serving other gods.' Joshua warned them that it would not be easy to serve only Jahweh because he is a holy God and tolerates no other beside Himself. When the people insisted that they wished to serve only Jahweh, he called upon them to destroy all the idols they possessed.

Then came the surprising turn of events: Joshua fixed this covenant in a number of laws which he called the 'laws of God', and set up a stone under the oak in 'Jahweh's sanctuary'. Of course all he intended was to make the people's promise clear and concrete, a sign and a memorial. Joshua's intention was to improve the people's attitude towards God and their neighbours, but what he did in actual fact was to set up all the conditions for absolutising and sacralising a number of objects and norms. This is how in the long run, the holy scrolls of God's word came into existence and Jahweh himself, in spite of his many protests, was localised in the holy of holies of the holy temple in Jerusalem. Thus arose the institutionalised religion of 'Judaism' which defined personal and social behaviour right down to the smallest detail.

3. NATION

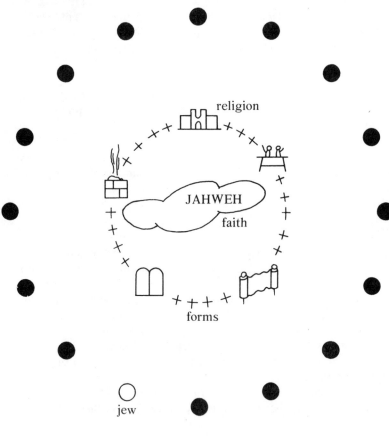

First and foremost of the mutual relationships which characterise the Jewish group is the blood relationship, which has been reinforced down the centuries by their common destiny. For the rest, their national bonds show the same characteristics as those of other nations: exclusivism, chauvinism, we-they thinking, which translated into religious terms was interpreted as we the chosen ones, superior to others. They tried to monopolise the God who wanted to be for all people.

Their uniqueness as a nation, the way they act, is largely determined by their life style and cultural pattern, which is completely interwoven with their religious pattern. The numerous feasts, rites, customs and prescriptions of their religion form the particular style of the education of their children.

Everyone understands that all these forms and rules were intended to mediate between the living group of believing Jews and the mystery of faith which united them. But we can become so attached and give so much 'value' to dead means of our own making that they obscure our view of the living relationship with God and erect a wall of holy things between the mystery and ourselves.

Human shapes, laws, norms, forms, holy things remained the tangible expression of their religious community but, at the same time, formed an obstacle to the experience of the true religious happening and prevented the encounter with religious values, with God. In Judaism too, time and again a prophet had to rise up to point out to the people that their faith in and understanding of Jahweh was darkened or totally eclipsed by all sorts of human forms of expression in their religion.*

4. *Christian Community*

Thanks to Christianity we know that God himself made a gesture to help us once and for all out of our continual backsliding inclination to declare holy the fabrications of our own mind and hand, and bowing down in worship before them.† Out of the depths of the divine mystery he stepped forth himself as a human being and dwelt among us. Those who lived at the time have related it to us and since then we can experience it ourselves. He took his place

*Adolf Exeler, 'Education and Catechesis', *Concilium* (English edition) 1970-3, pp. 34-42.
†Jurgen Moltmann, *Theology of Hope*, Harper and Row, New York, 1967.

among us in the human circle gathered around that mystery, which he called Father. In this way the old words (Exodus 20) became valid once more: 'I am your God. I am in the midst of you. Seek therefore no substitute for me.' With the coming of Christ the time of holy things and holy places and the sacralising of means should have been over for good, because he sanctified the human circle itself. This was how he lived and so he could say to us: 'What you have done to the least of mine (to anyone in the human circle), you have done to Me.' In Christianity it is no longer the holy things that matter, but the sanctification of people who are in a living relationship with the holy God.*

4. CHRISTIAN COMMUNITY

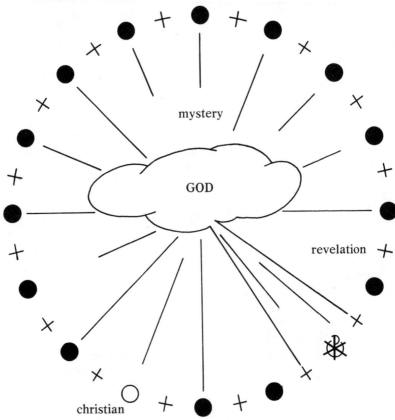

mystery

GOD

revelation

christian

*Jean Colson, 'The ecclesial ministries and the sacral', *Concilium* (English edition), 1972.

The early Christian Community was characterised by the living bond of each christian with the living Lord, sanctified by their new bond, their new covenant with God.

All who entered voluntarily were initiated into this mystery and taken up into the group of the faithful. The initiation of the children happened spontaneously through their participation with the adults.

5. *Church Denomination*

It is not surprising that even Christianity has not escaped man's innate need to enshrine his experience of the divine mystery in words and customs, rites, symbols and formulas. Christians too have regularly succumbed to the human weakness of trying to contain the mystery of our faith in laws and dogmas, and of attempting to localise God in holy places and in holy things.

We have canonised so many things: holy altar, holy church, holy see, holy cross, holy oil, holy doctrine and many similar things. There is no doubt that we cannot manage without a number of such expressions. They are useful means (signs and symbols) for the consecration of people and their togetherness, but the holiness of these things should never be given so much importance that people have to go on their knees before them or subject themselves to them. They should not form a barrier between the people and God. Yet in a number of mediaeval churches we actually see a screen placed between sinful man and the holy place called the sanctuary. Here too the same principle applies: all these things are secondary. The living people and the divine mystery, human behaviour and eternal values, the community of saints: these are primary.

It was Christianity that consistently spread among all nations the Jewish conviction of faith in God — the God of all nations. 'There is neither Jew nor Greek . . . neither slave nor free' says St Paul (Gal. 2:28). Christians are called together from all nations. 'Once you were no people, now you are God's people' (1 Pet. 2:10).

When the experience of the living bonds between people disappears, and is replaced by a number of rules and regulations that bind the members of a certain religion, the consequences are far more serious. Here there is no national bond, no cultural pattern to help people feel bound to each other as people.

This could be one of the reasons why Christianity split into so many denominations in the course of centuries. As a result either

5. CHURCH DENOMINATION

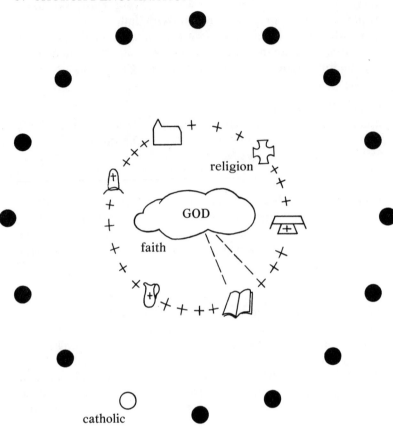

a national character and a religious pattern were combined to produce nations that were catholic, protestant or orthodox or, within the same country, gave rise to closed population groupings: the catholic group, the protestant group, the reformed group. That is how religious minorities maintain their identities.

Today these bonds of blood, of culture, of one's own group are rapidly disappearing. To many people today, being a Christian means being a member of a church denomination. They belong, and have rights and duties towards it, as in any organisation. And the obligations resulting from membership are enforced as, for example, compulsory attendance at Sunday Mass. A typical feature of this kind of church denomination is that a person comes not so much for *who* is there, but for *what* will be presented there. And that amounts to a sort of performance (put on by one person or by a small group) to which people come, round which they gather, with more or less interest. They are loosely bound, accidentally next to each other, without any feeling for each other.

This idea that it is a performance or a presentation is prevalent among many people. This is apparent from remarks like: 'It doesn't mean a thing to me any more' . . . 'It doesn't interest me any more', or as so many young people say: 'It is always the same.'

And if a church-goer does experience a real contact with the 'centre', the mystery, with God, then this is usually altogether incidental and personal. For many, the usual Sunday liturgy is seldom or never a warm group event, a communally experienced encounter with God.

And as far as the children are concerned: they have to be specially *instructed* in all the peculiarities of the church denomination — its theology, morality, exegesis. They have to 'learn' the faith. Adults say that children don't learn anything any more, but they themselves are not very clear about these things either.

6. *The Living Community of Faith*
Now we could go on and romanticise about the need to return to the primitive christian communities, but that would not be realistic. Twenty centuries of religious expression and christian culture cannot simply be discarded as useless.

What we have in mind in family catechesis is a combination of phase 4 and 5: a living christian community with the accumulated tradition of a church denomination. This seems to us to be a realistic goal. What is needed for this is the recreation of local living communities of faith. Therefore we opt for a catechesis of the relationships between the people in the outer circle and their relationship with God in their midst . . . an initiation of young and old into the mystery of our common destiny. This relationship catechesis will deal primarily with our relationships: I and YOU, I and OTHERS, founded in our bond with God in Jesus Christ. It will be about our belief in what joins us together, the communion and how we live it. Adults will draw the children with them into this. That is how they will be *initiated*; that means they may 'learn' to believe.

This catechesis differs from the usual instruction given by any denomination which teaches its own theology, morality and exegesis. Catholics normally teach christian dogma as Catholics interpret it, which means giving an explanation of our norms and forms, rites and customs, and showing how we catholics arrived at these in the course of time: i.e. the characteristics of our inner circle as Catholic church denomination. These are the usual content of catechesis and religious instruction and can be presented in many ways. But they are not primarily the content of family catechesis. Family catechesis wishes first to deal with the outer circle and with the centre, with our mutual relationships with each other and our relation to God. We really have no need to fear that the inner circle will never get a look-in again. Everything in it that can really function as a means to the end, as doors and windows through which we are enabled to meet God, will be brought up for discussion again.

For, as soon as a closer bond has grown among the faithful, as soon as their togetherness in God is more apparent, these relationships will demand forms of expression, celebrations, words, gestures, signs and symbols. There will be a demand for sacramental signs of this togetherness. Then the important thing will be: not again to present forms as 'holy' signs in isolation, but as sacramental signs, means man-made and therefore variable, and secondary to what is essential. What becomes of primary importance are our behaviour and the eternal value of our christianity, the sanctifying action of the living Lord, upon which his words, and all our theories and commentaries about him too, are based.

*Besides the general
Christian catechesis which
is currently focussing on
love of neighbour, family
catechesis highlights life as
sacrament.*

9. SACRAMENTAL CATECHESIS

1. By choice family catechesis is a sacramental catechesis. This could give cause for surprise in the light of what has been said already, but here we use 'sacramental' in the broad sense of 'life-consecrating' and not in the limited sense of sacralising ceremony.

   Used in its limited sense (and this is the sense that is still the most current and to which preparatory instruction 'catechesis' is usually confined) the sacramental event becomes, in our opinion, far too restricted to the moment of the sacramental celebration, while its relationship to personal life hardly figures at all.

2. The sacramental event should be understood in its widest sense, that is, as embracing the whole life of the believer — his being Catholic and how he practises this every day. This can be reinforced in the community by the celebration of the sacraments — such celebrations give life, new depth and significance. If nothing of the sacramental can be found in the life of people then there is nothing to celebrate. Family catechesis sees its first task as helping families to sanctify everyday life.

3. We often find that people who have taken part in family catechesis for a short while complain: 'You called us together to prepare for First Communion. But when are we going to get around to the actual sacrament?' They seem to be saying that it is about time that we started dealing with the doctrine of the sacrament, how it should be explained to children, particularly the sacramental ritual, what precisely it means and represents. But we are inclined to wait until very shortly before the actual celebration to deal with this.

Explanation of sacramental ritual is of little importance unless a far greater discovery has been made by all concerned. They must become aware that every sacrament has to do with their everyday life. Every sacrament aims at celebrating a mystery of life. This has first to be discovered, understood, grasped and experienced in faith if they are to celebrate it in faith. For religious education this implies that the content of a mystery of life (for example, communication and communicating with each other) must first of all take shape in the everyday life of each one individually both in their relationship with each other and with God. Without this it will have no meaning when celebrated as a sacrament. They will not be in 'the right state' (not in a 'state of grace' we used to say) to celebrate the sacrament.

On the whole, we are dealing with people who are not aware that the content of a sacrament is a particular mystery of life with which they are unconsciously occupied every day, a mystery which must first be experienced in faith if one wishes to celebrate it sacramentally. To them, the content of a sacrament is the ceremony, and they must know the meaning. Only then can they receive it. If children know that the host is Jesus himself, then they can receive communion. Hence the comment: 'I doubt whether our son is ready for his First Communion. Children know so little about it these days.'

Consequently during the parents' evenings, we find ourselves regularly faced with the tension between theory and practice, doctrine and life, law and conscience, norms and values. Our concept of the content of the sacrament is different from that which the people who come generally have. What they receive from us is a catechesis about their attitude to life and their faith, whereas they had expected to hear a number of little stories and hints to communicate to their children at home.

Fortunately, many of them still remember from earlier days that it used to be said even then: 'The seven sacraments are celebrations of the highlights of our lives.' Each sacrament is a religious celebration of a specific reality of life. That is how we as believers experience being born, walking along life's way, how we experience family and communication, going astray, failing and repenting, growing up and becoming mature, being of service and being appreciated, suffering and dying. If none of this happened in life, there would not be a sacrament for it either.

Once people have understood and experienced this sacramentally in some way, it is not difficult for them to recognise in the symbolism of the sacrament their own 'sacramental' experiences, which have indeed hallowed their life and the events of every day and given them a new dimension. The hallowing of life can now be meaningfully celebrated in the sacrament. Only now are people ready for this celebration, because only now have they come to appreciate, from their own experience, the fullness of its content and as a result 'the reception of the sacrament' can become a real celebration of a lived mystery of faith.

Too Sacred?

The hallowing of one's daily life is a concept which presents difficulty to a considerable number of Catholics today. 'We hardly pray any more. We don't go to church so often anymore . . .' are comments one often hears, as if these were the most important things. Two contrasting difficulties and objections, which are very real and which are regularly raised, need to be discussed. On the one hand we are told that we are making the profane too sacred; and on the other hand that we are making the sacred profane. To begin with, if we are hallowing profane life, how do we account for the secularisation of society today?

Whatever we may think of secularisation, if it has done anything at all it has freed human history from the grip of fate: from fate, whether it has a religious meaning or not, that enslaves people to the past and to the absolute authority of (often absurd) conventions and traditions. Secularisation has freed man from concepts of higher powers which, being hostile, could surprise or attack him, powers like Dame Fortune and the Fates, who held man at their mercy and subjected him to their whim.*

Secularisation has placed in people's own hands the responsibility for their own world and for what they would make of their own history.

We are taking secularisation in this sense a step further. We are not aiming at the sacralisation of profane forms present in society, such as official laws, prescriptions, regulations and patterns, since we know that these are always only human work conditioned by time and place. We are convinced that we must

---

*Harvey Cox, *The Secular City*, SCM Press, London, 1966.

continually pose questions, prompted by the gospel, about the value and authority of the whole contemporary scene and about the measures for which, according to the 'opinion makers', we are now deemed to be ready. We appeal to people not to allow themselves to be conditioned by this new style of 'fate', as though they were dealing with fixed and unquestionable patterns of life and unavoidable developments. We try to help each other to keep in our own hands the responsibility for our lives and for what we do.

This sacramental catechesis aims at putting every believer in a position where he can come, within the official framework of society, to a personal and conscious stand so that he knows how to direct his own life and his dealing with others, according to his personal convictions. For a believer this means that he knows how to hallow his life and his association with others on the basis of his personal faith in God. He tries to understand God's invitation in the people and the circumstances of this moment and he wishes to respond as perfectly as possible in a personal and believing way. He tries to follow the attitude of Jesus: 'My daily bread is to do the will of my father.' This 'will of the Father,' this meeting with the personal living God, did not come to him (and neither does it come to us) primarily through such things as structures, books, rules and dogmas, what we might call a 'pre-packaged' revelation.

The living revelation of God comes to us primarily in the realities of the moment, in the people and the values which demand an evaluation in faith here and now. Our response to this means the hallowing of that situation.

Faith in the living God means: faith in his living presence now, with these living people, and in these circumstances in which his living invitation reveals itself to me, and beside which all deposited and handed-down revelations are but secondary. These traditions are important, even indispensible in the long run, to the whole process of believing and being a Christian. But they are still only a means, and certainly not criteria which have priority over the here and now of God's invitation. In these people and in these circumstances God reveals himself in a completely new way to me, and asks for my believing cooperation if anything of his plan of salvation is to materialise in the history of man. My answer to him here and now is of the essence; of lesser importance is what may have been experienced about him previously and what has been written.

Think of this in terms of parents whose child confronts them with a situation which demands immediate attention. They do not go and consult a handbook first, to find out what they ought to do in such a case. They react spontaneously and to the best of their ability as human beings. Afterwards they may learn from a book how to do better next time.

Similarly we cannot keep people waiting while we page through the scriptures to see what God may require of us. In these people and in their situation, God himself is asking for an answer. The reading of scripture either before or after will be able to teach us a great deal and clarify much. Faith is not a question of standard reactions at fixed times but of wisdom and trust in God in the decisions of every moment.

In this context the remark of Don Bosco is significant: 'I have acted every moment as circumstances have required and as God inspired me'. . . Hence his statement 'Every moment is tremendously precious'. With secularisation the 'saeculum' has become all important . . . this age . . . our time. All that we possess is this moment, this brief instant of the here and now, so each one of us must discover that the *now* is vital.

We can interpret this in a limited sense merely by seeking to fulfil our human needs now or by bargaining with the supposedly higher power to fulful them for us. On the other hand we can view the importance of the here and now with the eye of the believer. This allows us to see it in a wider perspective, as an invitation from God which comes to us through these people and circumstances and which calls for a believing answer. By responding we become a cor-worker with God, a co-creator of this moment in a constantly changing world. Life then becomes a book of faith which we read and in which we ourselves also write.

Too profane?

In emphasising the primary importance of the present moment and this concrete life situation, we are bound to be accused of profaning the sacred, of keeping everything on too horizontal a level, of reducing everything to mere humanism. What is the extra dimension for the believer?

These objections stem from a misunderstanding of our catechesis. Judging by the topics we present for discussion and the practical results, it might seem that we have the same preoccupation or at least the same goal as humanists do. At first sight both the christian and the humanist are concerned with man's self-realisation through devotion to the welfare of his fellowmen.

The humanist stays within the circle. He acts solely for his own sake and the sake of his fellowmen. The christian also acts for the sake of himself and his neighbours, whom he wants to love as himself, but he does so in the deeper realisation that it is only in this way that he can love God above all. Thus he opens up the closed circle of the human, and the horizontal takes on height and depth. There is therefore a clear distinction between humanism and christianity.

In the encyclical *Populorum Progressio*, Pope Paul VI speaks of a narrow closed humanism without God, by contrast with which he calls christianity 'an open humanism, open to God' (no. 42). It is striking that he gives both these approaches the name of humanism. This is a good thing, because it is not a question of one being right and the other wrong, of opposing each other, but rather of appreciating and respecting each other, because we have much in common. If we ask a humanist how he can bring himself to devote himself to the welfare of humanity, no matter how hopeless, uncertain or oppressive a situation may be, he will say it is because he has learned to live with uncertainties. We hear the same answer from Christians. To stop there, is to be a humanist. To a believer, the acknowledgement by an unbeliever of the uncertain, is an indication that he is not dealing in fantasy but is facing reality. This diagnosis of a situation in which we live but which transcends us as human beings, over which we have no control, seems to be experienced by all men as something mysterious. All of us are faced with a reality which is larger than ourselves. But the humanistic view of life says still more about what a person actually can experience in his life, even if he feels no need to find the explanation for it. A person who has learned to live with uncertainty (and he is not the person who is always talking about it) will have learnt from experience that a situation that seemed threatening has often opened out a new direction in his life, once he takes the risk of submitting himself to it and making the most of it. In this way he learns, purely from his human experience, to have confidence and trust in the final outcome of events. Henceforth uncertainty no longer has such a paralysing effect on him.

That is how he learns to 'live with uncertainty'.

Every Christian can have the same experience in his life, since in faith he meets every human reality in the natural human way. But a believer does not stop at these human values. He looks for the deeper ground on which they are based and learns to perceive the situation which confronts him as an invitation to which he tries to respond to the best of his ability. The fact that a complex situation begins to sort itself out and is miraculously resolved is experienced by him as the work of God.

In the long run this means that a believer does not approach the uncertainties of life with uncertainty. He knows as little as any humanist how things will turn out in the end, what the next moment will bring or how he will come through it. The situation which faces him is just as uncertain for the christian as for any other person. In this sense the believer must also dare to risk and be able to live with risk. But his assessment of an obscure situation, his attitude in the midst of fearful events, his interior state, is actually not that of a totally uncertain person or someone who has learned to cope with the uncertain on purely human grounds. No matter what may befall him, he will always retain his inner trust and certainty because of his faith in God. Facing the uncertain is experienced and understood by him as something that happens under God's eye, granted by him or asked by him who knows all about it, a situation to which he can resign himself with a certain peace of mind, that enables him to cope with it.

This is what has always been called living in the presence of God. It gives the believer the inner certainty to accept his life situations, to face them as they come upon him and to put them to the best use to make his life holy and so to contribute to the coming of the kingdom of God.

It is this openness to the 'third person in the covenant', which gives him the certainty of faith that he is able to make of his life a redeeming event now and for always, that is the difference between the christian and the humanist.

'In the bible the Hebrew word for "believe" is also the word for "trust". Belief is trusting in life, trusting in people, trusting in oneself.

The basis of this trust is the covenant between God and man. The realisation of this covenant, our trust, and therefore our faith, increases with the perception that our covenant with our fellowmen and with all of reality is rooted in our covenant with God. And in this way God is the real, though usually unperceived, ground on which everything in life is based, which supports everything and makes everything possible' (Mgr Bluyssen, Bishop of Den Bosch).

*A man built his house upon
sand. The storm came and
it collapsed. A man built his
house upon rock. The storm
came. It remained standing.*

10. CATECHESIS AND SCIENCE

(See Table I, The Three Dimensions of Reality p. 80)

Matthew's image of the house built on sand that collapsed, and
the house built on rock which remained standing, puts in a few
words what we consider to be the criterion of religious education.
In Table I, we have tried to present a summary of what we mean
by this. In this chapter, we give a detailed explanation of our
interpretation.

[Roman numerals refer to the vertical columns in Table I and
arabic numerals indicate the horizontal levels.]

I Three dimensions

For the believing person every reality has three dimensions:
1. the data

2. the foundation upon which it rests

3. the deepest ground of its existence.
(1 and 2 can be perceived by everyone; 3 only by believers)

II Reality — form of existence

1. The data of a given situation is the concrete, tangible, directly
    observable phenomena of this very moment, the here and now
    — in other words what we call 'reality'; for example the fact
    that we see bread. We observe an obvious fact and we acknow-
    ledge it by stating 'that is bread'.

I. DIMENSION	II. REALITY — FORM OF EXISTENCE	III. VIEWPOINT — VISION	IV. STANCE — ATTITUDE		V. SCIENTIFIC APPROACH
			individual	social	
					auxiliary sciences
1) Data	the actual here and now reality BREAD observing stating the fact	directly visible observable "ordinary" human everyday obvious superficial	BEHAVIOUR Me deeds	the others BEHAVIOUR style, fashions moulding appearance practice trade, profession economy, industry politics sport, etc.	content of: joint subjects Question: who, what? where, which? Answer: information
2) Foundation HUMAN LEVEL	is based on a subsoil: culture LIVING: by and for each other reflecting interpreting - - - - the object of human (scientific) approach	what lies behind background "deeply" human reason, explanation deeper meaning - - - - context links life pattern	NORMS rules laws customs traditions - - - - HUMAN VALUES place-, time-, nation-linked	structure, system lines, links theory ideology that cultural pattern - - - - religious pattern doctrine, scripture, rite church organisation the faith, the hope THE MANY WAYS OF PEOPLE	culture lesson society lesson Question: in connection with whom? what? which? Answer: formation religion lesson phenomenology philosophy anthropology sociology psychology
3) Deepest ground DIVINE MILIEU	sand? rock? Mt. 7:21-27 on which the foundation itself rests: BREAD OF ETERNAL LIFE searching faith only to be approached in faith	deepest dimension deepest meaning, mystery Invisible revelation of the Deepest Being, God Good Tidings GOD'S WORD Disposition of Christ: MADE MAN	ETERNAL VALUES I the self experience faith in the absolute hope in the ultimate love for God members of God's People in Christ subservient to God's Kingdom living in God's presence universal	in the relationships the OTHER and the experience of the other THE WAY OF GOD UP TO HERE FOR EVERYONE	can be come CATECHESIS Question: why? to what purpose? Answer: meaning, praxis gift and account theology: moral exegesis pastoral each one puts different questions ABOUT THE SAME THING

Table I: The Three Dimensions of Reality

2. However, reality rests on the fact that each member in a specific group regards a number of things as normal because they belong to his culture. There is an overall pattern of human regulations and insights which explains daily phenomena: for example plain ordinary bread not only stands for a large number of human discoveries and developments but, at least in our part of the world, is the symbol of the human reality that we depend on each other for life . . . that we live by each other and for each other. Here already it is not just a matter of observing and recognising, but much more of reflecting and interpreting. A child does not see the connection at once. It demands a certain maturity to understand this human depth in the observation of ordinary bread. This can be scientifically explored, proved and taught. It is the object of a scientific approach.

3. If we now ask why this is so, what the deeper meaning is, what is the ground or foundation on which this human reality is based, we can arrive at two different views of the same reality. To restrict ourselves to the purely human sphere, to what is of a passing nature, or occupy ourselves only with the here and now, explaining everything on rational grounds, is for the believer like building on sand. If however our edifices, with the human foundations, are based on our faith in God who builds with our hands, then we are building on rock. Or as the psalmist says: 'Unless the Lord builds the house, those who build it labour in vain' (Ps 126). To return to our example: when, apart from the fact of bread itself we have also understood the underlying human law that we live by and for each other, then (and only then) can we become aware of the deepest consequences of what is revealed in the 'Bread of Eternal Life', Christ himself, who gives himself as food. Then to see this in the Eucharist is no longer a result of arguing about transubstantiation, but of a searching faith. Here we enter the divine dimension, the divine milieu which can only be approached in faith.

III Viewpoint — vision

We are always dealing with the same reality. But at every level there is a different viewpoint.

1. Many people live very superficially. They look only at the surface. They do not go much deeper. The 'looking' of the young in particular remains mostly limited to the directly visible and observable, the ordinary obvious everyday human things. And indeed, looked at superficially, things are as they see them: 'I eat bread when I am hungry. And that's all there is to it.'

2. But sooner or later a person begins to use his intelligence and asks what lies behind observable reality, how it all came about. Or that question confronts him once he starts dealing with other people. Then questions about what lies under the surface, about the 'deeply human' which gives the reason and explanation for people acting in a particular way, are bound to come up. Here we are on the level of the human context. This context is not immediately visible but it links the things we regularly see and do, making of them a rounded life pattern within which the individual is able to operate.

3. The believer, however, is not satisfied with purely human explanations whatever they may be, because they leave all the real questions unsolved for him, questions about the deepest dimension of things, about 'why' everything is arranged as it is. In this way throughout the centuries people have come face to face with the mystery, the invisible; they were not able to come into direct contact with it, but they could notice its traces in nature and creation and in the great signs in the heavens and on earth. In Judaism and in Christianity the experience has been that the deepest sorce of Being reveals himself to us as the One Living God who speaks to us in his works. For the Christian it is the Word of God that was made flesh in the person and dispositions of Jesus Christ. That is the good news. God is near us; he lives among us. He has taken his place in the circle of human beings.

IV Stance — attitude

The stance each person adopts in respect to reality depends largely on the group from which he comes, the people among whom he finds himself and the values which he regards as important.

1. What we do and how we behave are not in most cases the result of the relationship between 'me and this thing', they are not individual occurrences but, more often, social occurrences, a moulding of relationships: 'me and the other people around this thing.' In every group there appear differences in behaviour, styles and fashions peculiar to the group. These distinguish this group from other groups. This affects the image of specific societies. It leads, for example, to trades and professions which differ from country to country. Even in the same society there is a distinct difference between the behaviour of a 'trades-man' and the behaviour of a 'sportsman', for example.

2. There is a reason for these differences. People do it 'this way' for a specific reason. They base their actions and behaviour on specific theories about development and association of which they themselves are aware or which others have perceived before them: on these they construct an ideology or philosophy which gives rise to structures and systems accepted by the group: to cultural patterns, to codes of professional ethics. From these communal insights have developed a number of norms, laws, rules and customs for the behaviour of individuals. They are very clearly bound to time and place and to the group from which they stem. These are the many different forms of human culture and society. (Reflection III)

N.B. We would like to point that that every religious pattern can likewise be seen as a facet of a specific culture or grouping. Most religions have all the necessary attributes: their own special norms and rites, their secrets, doctrine, writings, and their church organisation. Besides their personal attitudes of belief and hope, people often speak of *the* faith and *the* hope as though these were abstract realities which could be defined in a few words. All these norms and systems, religious ones included, remain human forms. As such we can make them the object of scientific study. In their pluriformity and variety they simply reveal the cultural or religious ways of people. To study them is to engage in a human activity.

To limit oneself to this, for example in education, is, in the eys of the believer, like building on shifting sand. However it must be kept in mind that at birth every human being is set upon one of these many religious ways. This is inevitable.

3. The believer thinks he must dig deeper. He is convinced that, beneath all these formal differences of a temporary nature, lie hidden lasting *values* which are valid for all people. These values are not visible, but they are indirectly made visible in forms and actions. That is why one can look for them in all the forms people have given to them over the centuries as well as in the daily actions and omissions of every person. In these days, however, we can not simply take it for granted that these values do lie hidden there. For far too long this has been considered self-evident. Young people are not without reason when they complain: 'Our parents are constantly telling us what we must do and must not do. When we ask why, they don't even know themselves.' 'That's the way it has always been!' is no longer a satisfactory answer.

Norms are unable completely and adequately to express the richness of a value. It can happen that the norm-system starts to lead a life of its own, it no longer derives its right of existence from the value which gave it shape, but rather from the power and authority of some body which now justifies and safeguards its own position by reference to the norm itself. Then it is clearly to their advantage that the situation is never questioned or put under scrutiny, for fear that the existing balance of forces will be upset.

So there are countless reasons why norms can degenerate and why human forms of expression can obscure the vision and inhibit the practice of these values, instead of enabling them to be realised — which is what they were designed for in the first place, and what they most probably did contribute toward initially.

Instead of accepting norms as sacred, untouchable absolutes, the person of true faith will continually test them against their real value. That is, first and foremost against this living reality, the living association of me with other men, at this moment, with God in our midst. This awareness of God's presence holds an invitation to me and to all men, an invitation that begs an answer to give it meaning.

From this point of view, the individual never stands alone. The deepest values are to be found primarily in the relationships in which each individual stands at every moment: the experience of self and the experience of the other, and within this our common experience of the Other, God in Jesus Christ, who regards whatsoever is done to the smallest and least in this society as done to Himself. That is why in our analytical chart we have made no distinction between myself and others as far as our stance in respect of values is concerned. Even if a person is able to see his own behaviour apart from the behaviour of society (1) and can distance his own theories and experience of norms from the official structures and ideologies (2) the deepest values can only be found by the human being in his love of God and in treating his neighbour as himself, moment by moment. 'Where two or three are gathered in my name, there am I in their midst'. . . (Mt 18:20).

It is given only to the believer to adopt such a stand. Then he knows himself to be taken up in God's milieu, and this gives him a great inner security and peace, a firm trust in the happy outcome of everything which makes him anxious or threatens him. He knows that he is contributing to the building up of God's Kingdom with everything that he may now be or do.

The believer sees this attitude to life as the deepest universal reality, the eternal value for all people, the one and only way of all human kind towards God. Just as a person is by his birth set on one of the many human ways, so by his baptism he is being set on the one and only way of all mankind to God. From this we must also deduce that all who meet each other in this vision and attitude of faith possess true living faith. Together they make up God's people on the way, whatever form of expression they may give to it.

This leads to an important conclusion: this is especially the task of every christian. We think that everything we have said up to now can be achieved and can be lived out by everyone; and that each and every 'layman' can put it into practise in christian witness. It is primarily here that we find the task of christian education for parents and educators. This is the catechesis of reality, of life in which everyone gives his own account of faith, something which he must be considered capable of doing.

V The scientic approach

That last conclusion leads naturally to the question of the relationship between catechesis and science, between 'layman' and
specialist.

1. The observation and study of all kinds of observable data is
   the primary content of a number of so-called profane disciplines.
   At this level the questions asked are: where, which, what, when,
   how much and how? And the answer is a specific amount of
   information, which can be measured and verified. Typical ways
   of testing this kind of knowledge are quizzes, puzzles and
   objective tests. There are teachers of religion who see merit
   in treating facts about the Bible, the holy land, church history
   or doctrine in this way and requiring its reproduction in tests.

   It will be quite clear that in our opinion, this has nothing
   to do with catechesis or religious education.

2. At a deeper level than these concrete data and phenomena
   we come to the particular field of cultural and social formation.
   Here we must immediately note that people's basic human
   associations and judgements, their philosophy of life, continually play a part in all the other disciplines that they engage
   in.

   Obviously at this level quite different questions are asked.
   Now they are questions of relationships: with whom, or in
   which context, have these things been arranged by this particular group of people?

   To answer requires reflection and interpretation. That is
   the only way one can learn to see the context in which different
   cultures and civilisations have been formed. It requires insight
   into all sorts of opinions and backgrounds to be able to explain
   why people have arrived at particular cultural expressions.

   Before anyone is in a position to give an answer at this level,
   he must have had proper guidance in the formation of his
   personality and the deepening of his thought-process. Sciences
   that are helpful in the area of cultural and social formation
   are, inter alia: phenomenology; philosophy; anthropology;
   sociology and psychology.

   In IV, 2 above, we said that the religious pattern may remain
   on a purely human, cultural level. Here we must add that

religious instruction, when seen merely as the objective teaching of one's own religious pattern or of other religions, will find itself confined within the human approach to human facts. The name suggests that it is concerned with God; yet it is *about* God while God is absent from it. His living presence and his activity in the reality of the present moment is kept completely out of it. He himself is kept out of it. There is no difference between such a 'religion' lesson and any other lesson on cultural history.

3. On the other hand a religion lesson which begins on that level, and even a lesson which begins with cultural or social formation, can gradually deepen into real catechesis. Although one is dealing with the same reality, the questioning penetrates to the deepest ground and is immediately directed at people here and now as they stand in this reality. We are no longer asking: 'What do we see here?' and no longer: 'How did people arrive at this or that?' The questions now become: 'Why is this or that the way it is?' 'What does it mean and what is it for?' 'What does it lead to?' and each time 'What meaning does it have for me?'

Now the instrument in the search for an answer is no longer the observing or reasoning intelligence, but the seeking in faith, the hopeful looking forward and the trusting in the love of God.

This is the only way to find an answer which shows reason and meaning and at the same time invites us to give that answer. Because to see the reason, to understand God's invitation, requires us to give that answer immediately and to give it that meaning. Otherwise nothing happens at all.

The aim of catechesis in this sense is always twofold: theoretical as well as practical, the vision of faith and the attitude of faith. It is a matter of making people aware and of clarifying what they do so that they can come to a better living of it.

Exegesis, dogma, moral and pastoral theology, catechetics etc are ancillary sciences to the training given by a specialist-catechist. They serve the catechist as a basis to back up what he teaches. They do not form the primary content of his cate-chesis. They are scientific and therefore human expressions of the reality of faith. They are human concepts, thought-images. As such they belong to level 2 of human cultural advancement.

This does not deny that they can become catechesis and proclamation at the moment when they bring good tidings of liberation and redemption to people. But at that precise moment strict formal treatment of the content of any of these religious sciences is abandoned.

The conclusion of this synopsis seems clear: in everything, and at every level, we are concerned with the same reality and with every dimension of it. But at each level people have a different understanding of reality, they adopt a different attitude to it and ask different questions about it.

Photo: Michael Shinners

Photo: Michael Shinners

PART III
THE COMMUNION PROJECT

The most striking thing about this project is perhaps the spontaneous shift which is taking place from the priest-centred church to the lay-centred church.

N.B. The material for this Communion project consists of:
* a file for parents (with ideas and suggestions for the home)
* suggested worksheets for children
* a file with suggestions, models and aids, for parish catechesis.

* *The time is ripe* for going more deeply into the problems which worry us daily. This can help everyone find his way and become aware of the meaning of his own life (p. 94).

* We can be of *help to each other in our decision making.* What God wants of each individual is revealed in this living moment, in our meeting with our fellow men. For believers this is the meaning of our communion in Christ (p. 100).

* *Preparation* for First Communion *motivates* people to get together. People facing similar problems can help each other and can learn what a joy it is when young and old are able to communicate with each other (p. 104).

* If we really want people to make a good decision we must *start early* (p. 108).

* The *parents' evening* is a religious meeting of people on the way 'towards a living church'. For parents it is a chance to prepare themselves for a deeper questioning of their own actions and also of the lives of their children. This means pushing beyond their normal limitations, knowing that with God's help, this is possible (p. 110).

* Experience is gained as parents become involved in doing the project's *practical work*, using the file and preparing the celebrations (p. 115).

* The *structure* of the project hinges on the experience of daily life, of nature and of the church's year (p. 119).

* Those responsible for the communion project soon discover that they have begun something exciting. The way of doing it, as well as the project itself, is important. There should be a *division of labour* so that the laity are involved both in the organisation and in the pastoral tasks (p. 123).

* In Family Catechesis the *project* and the *process* must be linked. In the first phase parents are helped to become family catechists. In the second phase a number of participants develop into pastoral co-workers. And in the third phase the demand for lay ministry formation becomes steadily more urgent (p. 131).

Your path in life is your own story of joy and sorrow interwoven with the story of Jesus and the stories of the many people who make up God's salvation history.

11. THE TIME IS RIPE

One thing that stands out in our society is that even the 'most sacred' rules and laws have become a matter for argument and have been deprived of their divine authority. People say this is because western society has grown up, become mature and independent. But if you look at what is really going on, you get the impression that the baby has been thrown out with the bath-water or at least that values have gone overboard along with the rules.

The strange thing is that not only the mass of people but even many leaders do not see these unfavourable developments in society in a mature and balanced light.

Rules seem to be swept away with such rancour that no one bothers to check whether the deeper foundations and values on which they were based actually demand a return to the same rules, or at least the establishment of rules based on those deeper values. One can hardly avoid the impression that, in a completely adolescent manner of 'long live liberty', all sorts of fashionable trends and superficial regulations are set up. These are clothed in a wealth of psychological, sociological arguments and rationalisations, but have little basis in the deepest layers of human existence and the mystery of human dignity. An enormous amount of theorising goes on but it has little lasting happiness to offer. Rest assured that many people will brand us as some kind of conservative for saying this.

What we are trying to voice is not pessimism but serious concern. There are many indications of the damage being done. Supposing someone were to write a history of the 70's. What would it read like?

The 70's

In the 70's people paid little attention to rules; they made changes but did so in a very odd way.

They were aware that in poor countries whole peoples regularly faced death from famine, drought, disease and natural disaster. So they set up relief agencies which kept the people alive — but they did not remove the causes.

They noticed that more and more marriages were breaking up because the partners could not remain faithful to each other and did not know how to make each other happy. So they made divorce laws easier — but they did not remove the causes.

They noticed that, as a result, children became the victims of the disturbed relations between parents. There was a worrying increase in the number of children who because of tensions at home, could not benefit from school. So they introduced a whole system of educational first-aid for these 'disturbed' children — but they did not remove the causes.

It was generally held that the individual should be able to live freely, to be himself, without restriction. But since, in exercising their own freedom, many people showed no consideration for others, others naturally became their victims. So all sorts of remedies were invented to suppress the inevitable results: pep-pills, tranquillizers, contraceptives, abortion clinics. In these ways they tried to plug the gaps they themselves had made — but they did not remove the causes.

As a result of all this it gradually became apparent that young adults remained extremely immature and unbalanced. These young people huddled together in parks, dressed strangely, took comfort in drugs and could not settle down. So these places were abandoned to the young people and drug usage was legitimised. When the situation got out of hand new regulations were made — but they did not remove the causes.

In the 70's the church was always wrong. If it ranged itself somewhat on the side of the powerful, it went without saying that it was completely wrong. If it joined the opposition it was equally wrong, and if it stayed neutral it was altogether irrelevant. The silence of the church in distant lands was severely condemned, but if at home she raised her voice against the superficiality of society which was endangering the health of the nation, then she was intruding on the freedom and rights of people to decide for themselves.

Because many people could not see their way clearly any more, they simply blundered along and, sooner or later, accepted these superficial solutions. They called this 'democratic decision-making'. If the majority was 'ready for it' (a matter of systematically hammering it in), then anything could be pushed through as acceptable. Alas, people in general were only too pleased with themselves and with what they had achieved. Everyone who 'could go along' with this course of action was called 'open', 'progressive'.

At that time there was no shortage of wise men, who knew how to go deeper into the background and show why these things were happening, but before they could open their mouths they were shoved into a corner and labelled 'authoritarian', 'conservative', 'fanatic' or 'narrow-minded'. (And, of course, some of them did deserve these labels.)

Eventually one out of every two adults was under some kind of stress. About 25% of young adults were clearly inadequate, with unresolved tensions and a very poorly developed ability to relate maturely to other people. (These figures relate to the Netherlands.)

Finding one's own way

It is too soon to say what will have been done about the situation by the end of the 70's. Will the causes have been removed by then?

We are not panicking or despairing — but we are appealing for some serious rethinking. We consider that the time is ripe for something to be done about the present state of affairs and we believe that we have a message for our time, good news, really joyful tidings. Once again we are finding our way, we are learning to delve deeply so that once more we can understand God's invitation in the circumstances of our lives.* Should our patterns and standards be variable? Yes, certainly, but not so as to unleash chaos. We must dare to risk the consequences of

*Andrew M. Greeley, *The New Agenda*, Doubleday, New York, 1973.

posing deeper questions in order to arrive at sounder rules and decisions. More definite standards are preferable to the disintegration and collapse of so many people.

Many people today find themselves in a dilemma. What should we do in the present state of confusion? Try to find our own way or stick to those things that religion says should be maintained? Jehovah's Witnesses boast a large increase in numbers of whom many, a great many, were formerly Catholics. 'Broad and easy is the way to destruction; straight and narrow is the way that leads to heaven': people still hear these words at the back of their minds and so they opt for the certain rather than the uncertain.

How important are the rules; what weight do the regulations carry — all ranks in the church want to know the answer. Is there such a thing as a compulsory way we must follow, are there compulsory steps we must take, prescribed practices we must carry out with our daily duties, or in addition to them? Are there obligations and duties we must perform because we are Catholics? Are there truths that we must know and defend to the death? Isn't it best to be on the safe side?

On the other hand the fact remains — and it has never been any different — that every man must make his own way through life. No man treads the same path as another.

Let us visualise the consequences if each man's path is always his own — the way to achieve his own happiness. Then there would be so many ways, each different, sometimes difficult to find, but still for each his own way: a very narrow and uncertain way, because no one else has ever walked it. It is travelled only once.

This is the reverse side of the coin, which is just as real. This is the individual dilemma before which we all stand. Either we renounce our personal decisions of conscience and allow ourselves and our actions to be programmed according to systems set up by others, or we retain the right to act for ourselves and seek our own way.

One's own story

Once we decide to go our own way, the question is: 'How do we decide?' 'On what do we base our decision?' We forget that for

Christians the question should really be: 'On whom is that decision based?'

For us the way is not *something*, some factual data, but *Somebody*, Jesus, who said of himself: 'I am the way, the truth and the life.' At the crossroads where we stand, it means so much if we experience Jesus as the Living One who is near us.

In the first place, this means that the way and the truth is not a doctrine about God or about heaven, recorded in books. It is not an institution to be defended. It is a Person. Seeking one's way is seeking him; finding one's way is meeting him. Jesus does not say: I know the way, I have the truth, but: I am the way, the truth.

This is a biblical manner of speaking which has much to say to us in these depersonalised times. Where we work in terms of dogmas and dead ideas, where we use nouns and abstractions, the bible speaks of living realities, of a presence, and uses verbs. It does not describe what something is, but how it fits into creation, into mankind. For example, it calls something 'true' if it can be relied upon. A vine that bears fruit is a true vine. The true God means: he does what he has promised. He is faithful to his word. He is truthful. In the bible, action is the barometer of truth. The New Testament goes still further. There truth is a person. God's word has become true in this person. It has become flesh in Christ who said of himself: I am the truth, that is, I make God's meaning completely true in my life; to find God, happiness, heaven, you do things this way.

The biblical way of asking is not: What is this or that? but, How do you do that? Then follows a story about a person and the way he did it.

The bible never talks about faith, but about believing. That is the story of Abraham, the father of all believers: that is how you should believe. The story of Moses is about being faithful. The story of King David is about growing by responding to God's call. And loving? That is the story of Jesus.

When Jesus said of himself: 'I am the way, the truth and the life' he meant: I have realised God's intention in my life, I have found the way, I have achieved happiness.

Therefore the attitude of Jesus towards people and his relationship with God is the true foundation, the deepest value for every christian; meeting him is the real way which leads to true life for everyone.

The individual way of each person is his own story. This, interwoven with the story of Jesus and the countless stories of mankind, constitutes the history of salvation.

To decide is always to surrender, either to certainties which were once established, or to the living Lord in the encounter of this moment.

12. HELPING EACH OTHER TO DECIDE

Because we want to be really concrete and practical, we must ask ourselves: What are we to do when we realise that the deepest value for us who believe is Christ, the living Lord in our midst? He is our way — the way each one of us can go with him. But what does this say to the man in the street? Situations crop up when he must decide whether to do something or not to do it. How does he decide? What does he choose? Where can he consult Christ? Where does he meet him?

At this point a very strange thing happens. Many believers take flight from the living moment, from the living Christ, and seek refuge in books and writing about him. They seek no original, living answer to the living question, but frantically try to treat the new question with a scholarly or routine answer. They have had a theory imprinted upon their minds and it still remains: Christ comes to us in the books of holy scriptures and in the doctrine, laws and prescriptions of the church. That is true in a secondary sense. But in the first instance, it cannot be true. That is not the experience of the church now, nor was it in earlier times — life transcends book learning.

The living Christ is not merely indirectly in our midst through the medium of books and models from the past, but he is directly present and alive in the reality of this very moment: God with us. Catholic catechesis has always been more of a sacramental catechesis than a catechesis of the word and the scriptures.

But again, how does his living presence help us to make the right decisions? How can we communicate with him? Many Catholics today do not know which way to turn. At first they went along with the idea of 'God's people on the way' travelling the uncertain trail through the desert of the last ten years. But now more and more of them want to return to the fleshpots of Egypt: 'At least we knew where we were and what was what.' . . .

They seek certainty by demanding clear pronouncements from their bishops or from Rome, and also by measuring the content and value of a catechesis according to the amount of scripture and exegesis it contains.

However, to make a decision is, and always will be, to take a risk, to surrender to the uncertainty of wondering whether one is making a good choice or not.

How did things happen before? It is often said that in the past decisions were made either through social pressure or because the church had made things compulsory under penalty of sin. The reaction of people today is usually: well, in the past, people did not decide for themselves. They had no choice. They were treated like children and everything was decided for them. Now at least people have some freedom, everyone has room to make his own decisions.

Is this really so? Was everything so cut and dried before? True, the church made the laws, and they were impressed on people at an early age. And then there was the sacrament of confession: this gave them an opportunity to test their behaviour and the decision they had made in the light of the laws. It was also an opportunity to hear from a fellow-believer how he judged their decision and to consult him about the best decision to make. In this way consciences were formed. Above all, this fellow-believer was a priest, the sign par excellence for these people that Christ was present and spoke to them. People who were used to confession in this way experienced, then as now, that the living Lord could show them the way and help them in their personal decisions.

The practice of this sacrament has deteriorated seriously over the years. It has practically fallen into disuse. But has this improved matters in any way? Is there in fact such 'freedom', such 'room' for each to make his own decisions, as people say? Does modern man really decide for himself?

We meet an increasing number of people who are at a loss. They will not face up to things. They prefer to await developments. So they let things run their course, then they get out of hand and something drastic has to be done: 'The child will have to leave home and live elsewhere and we will just have to ask for a divorce.'

They do this, not because they had made up their minds long ago or because they intended to act like this, but because they find themselves faced with a fait accompli.

Is there really more room for individual decision? There is a lot of talk about tolerance, but are we really so tolerant?

Let parents venture to oppose anything that is called 'young or modern', anything that is 'the in-thing for people today' and they are immediately labelled 'backward, square, stupid, dull, narrow-minded'. Do these people have to examine their attitudes with a continual anxiety at the back of their minds: What will people think of me, what will they say about me, if I go on doing this or that, if I go on as I have always done? What is left of all that room for manoeuvre? How much freedom do we allow older people among us?

As for the younger ones, do they really decide for themselves? There are so many crazes, super-this, super-that. It's the thing to wear jeans, so everyone wears jeans. How can they go against what is the 'in-thing' for their peers? Talk about social control! They have to rave about the latest commercial on the radio or on T.V. or whatever the disc jockey says is top of the pops.

Many people have the feeling that we are in chaos. When it comes to individual decision-making, we must distinguish between three groups. At one extreme we have the rather small group of people who cling fanatically to the past. At the other extreme we have the small group who can understand the new developments, consciously choose and live them. And somewhere in the middle is the large group which lets things ride over them — they tend to wait and see. In the final analysis everything is being decided for these people, and arbitrarily at that.

The pastoral approach to communion

In their heart of hearts, many people are dissatisfied with the present state of affairs. Many young people are anxiously asking themselves: 'Has life so little meaning? Is this all there is to it?' The large group in the middle desperately needs someone to reach out a hand to them. So a whole new style of pastoral care is coming into existence. It is the work of people who want to help each other come to a genuine decision, at least at a few of the important moments of their lives, instead of just letting things run their course.

People who arrive at such moments of decision, generally have similar questions, anxieties and uncertainties. But they do not know this. Each one is worried about it, often burdened with it, but does not know where to turn to find clarity in his doubts. This is often complicated by shame, a feeling of guilt, rancour, bitterness: but perhaps most of all by confusion and a sense of helplessness.

Something wonderful often happens when these people get together to talk about the important questions which are bothering them. To their surprise, they find others struggling with the same difficulties. They can identify with the questions others raise, they feel reassured, comforted, understood and encouraged. They go home, taking the experience of the disciples on the road to Emmaus with them. 'Did not our hearts burn within us while we talked with each other?' It is the experience of the Lord being in our midst, of being on the way towards a living Church.

In this way people help each other to meet him, and in company with him and with each other to make a sound decision. This cannot be done on one's own. In this way christians of our time can learn to meet Christ at other moments of the day, at home or at work.

The most striking thing about this development is the spontaneous shift which is taking place here from the priest-centred church to the lay-centred church. This is a shift from the office-bearer who seemed to be the only one responsible for the formation of the consciences of the people, to the church of the laity where the faithful, seeking together and serving each other, find the way: find Christ and in doing so form their own consciences. In this way, decision-making does not become a surrender to certainties which were established once for all, but rather a surrender to the living Lord in the encounter of this moment.

We must first learn communion with him by living it with each other, before we are able really to celebrate it together.

*At certain times in their
lives people find themselves
faced with a decision
which leaves them baffled.
Family catechesis tries to
help them come to a sound
decision.*

13. THE MOTIVATION

The preparation of the child for 'First Holy Communion' is not
the primary goal of the whole communion-project. The heart
of our religion is living communion. Faithful members of the
believing community are often only too pleased to have a communion-project which offers a clear, instructive and fresh
approach to the religious education of their children. They benefit
from it too. They experience it as an enriching year in the faith-life
of their family and it is crowned by the celebration of the first
communion of one or more of their children.

The notion of 'first' communion, which is part of our tradition,
is sufficient motivation for parents to be interested.

Many baptised Catholic parents, who perhaps have scarcely
been to church for years, are faced with a moment of decision
which leaves them completely baffled. In general, these parents
are worried lest their children should grow up without religion.
They would feel easier if their children knew at least something
about religion, if they could still go to church through the school.
In their heart of hearts, they still consider the first communion
of their children important enough to make a real feast of it. They
do not want to deprive them of this. Now that the school no longer
prepares children for it, they must do it themselves. They seem
to appreciate being helped in this situation.

Pastors and practising christians may well have come to the
conclusion that the making of FIRST communion is not in fact
desirable as it is all fuss and completely meaningless. Yet it
would be pastorally wrong to do away with it or to play it down
altogether. This would be wasting an opportunity; such drastic
action on our part would not be helpful to most people. It would

only give them the feeling that something else was being 'taken away', something to which they had previously learned to attach great value. They would not understand why we were doing it.

By starting from the value which, deep down, they are still attached to, we can at least offer them a chance to realise for themselves what is essential in our communion with Christ. Celebrating this communion together is never a meaningless undertaking, and neither is the preparation of children to participate in communion festively, whether for the first or for any other time.

So the communion-project becomes a catechetical family project 'on the occasion of the preparation of the child for the feast of (first) communion'.

Aim

The particular aim of the project is:

to equip and assist parents to understand and to experience anew the reality of communicating in faith with each other in Christ;

to celebrate this with the whole believing community;

and finally, to celebrate the fact that their children also share and participate in it.

This approach does not presuppose a duty or an obligation which parents are bound to fulfil. Our pastoral approach is intended only to help parents clarify their situation so that at a given moment they may be able to take a real and responsible decision: yes or no, if that is what it is to be.

N.B. We do hope with this approach to begin to remove the 'magic threshold' idea, so that the strange separateness of the 'first' communion may gradually become a thing of the past. To illustrate this: During a family celebration that was part of our catechesis, young Paul said to his mother: 'Mum, I'm going to communion too.' His mother's first reaction was to say: 'No you can't! You haven't made your first communion yet!' To which Paul replied: 'But we have started.' So when his mother received the host from the priest, she broke off a little piece and gave it to Paul. Later, when the day of the celebration came, he would receive the host from the priest himself. (This was common practice in the early church — even for babes in arms).

Misuse?

Sometimes a different objection is raised against the structure of the communion-project. We are told that we are using the children, even misusing them, to reach the parents. People suggest that this is a dishonest approach, a kind of blackmail. This remark is often made by people who don't generally object to the use of the tactic in other contexts. Has it not been the accepted thing for people from church, state or any other institution to try to influence children through the parents? We all regard it as normal to go through parents or through authorities. This approach could also be questioned. It is just as one-sided and authoritarian. The communion-project works more on the principle of communication, that is a process of mutual influence whereby the child educates his parents just as much as he is educated by them. We think we can be of service to parents and children alike. As we can help the parents with the education of their children, so also we can create opportunities and possibilities for the child and we can lead parents to further development.

Our intention in providing this opportunity is to render a service to both parties, through the parents and through the children, so that they have a better relationship with each other and with God.

Proven method

This pastoral approach was developed by Don Bosco who said: 'You win the hearts of the adults by being good to their children.'

He gained this insight in a 'Mission dream' which he had about 1870. 'I saw savages storming over an enormous open plain. They fought against soldiers dressed like Europeans. Many lay dead on all sides. Then I saw missionaries arrive. I did not know any of them. They tried to go up to the savages, but they charged at them like men possessed and trampled them underfoot. I thought to myself: 'What can one do for such barbaric people?' Then I saw a different group of missionaries arrive. They were laughing and a large group of children frolicked around them. These were our people! I wanted to restrain them. Then, to my surprise, I saw that they were received with joy by those same men who had been raging killers a short while before.'

What became a proven method for the missions could very well turn out to be successful for the missionary task of the church in the modern world.

Acceptance

In many places First Communion is still called 'acceptance.' This meant the initiation of a child into the adult believing community. The child could now belong. The grown-ups already belonged to the parish, and the town or city. Our communion project shifts the accent from the child to the whole family, so we see an interesting change taking place in the meaning of 'acceptance'. Because so many people move house so often and because of the alienation which is common in cities and towns, families can live for years in a parish or neighbourhood without being part of the local community of faith or of the parish. This communion project can mean an initiation into the parish for a family. It is not just the admittance of one child, but also of the parents and the other children. In the course of a year the family can be accepted into the parish community and feel at home there.

There is another thing to be considered. First Communion is an occasion for the whole family. It involves not only the older brother or sisters who have already 'made their First Communion' but the younger children as well. It is not realistic therefore to repeat the performance a year or so later with the same family because a younger brother or sister is now of age. If we really see the communion project as the admittance of the whole family into the local community of faith, it becomes a celebration for all, and the little brother or sister who is only a year or two younger is in fact celebrating first communion as well. Having once been accepted as a practising family, there are enough new opportunities for old and young alike to be active in parish life and then be guided further.

In order to keep all these possibilities for development open, it is best to talk as little as possible about preparation for First Communion. We simply call it the communion project.

*We start talking about First
Communion in October?
First Communion doesn't
take place until May,
does it?**

14. STARTING EARLY

In the past the priest in confessional could always tell when
there was a First Communion somewhere in the neighbourhood.
At the last minute parents would come and confess; for years I
haven't practised, Father, but well . . . tomorrow my child is
making First Communion. They could not let their child down.
It is not so long since this kind of thing was happening. To avoid
this some parishes started to prepare parents ten days before
the event. Even if it were as long as two months, this seems too
short a time for parents to make important decisions. At that
stage they are too preoccupied about the celebration of the
sacrament, about whether their child will take part or not, how he
will get to know what the sacrament means, and how the celebration will be conducted. The parents' individual problems
and questions do not come up for discussion and the most
important part of the preparation, namely the more conscious
living-out of the mystery of faith in their daily activities, is simply
not dealt with at all.

We start in October in order to give parents time to consider
the consequences of their decision to let their child join in the
celebration of the first communion, or not.

The first reaction of many pastors is: 'From October to May
is far too long! It will never work with our people. You can't ask
them to do that, they will never persevere.' Fortunately most
pastors allow themselves to be persuaded to try it just once
and they soon become enthusiastic when they see how happy
people are with this approach; then they too become interested
and involved. When, for a good reason, parents do not come along,
they send apologies. Other parents take them the handouts they

*See Appendix I for alternative cycle (May-November) for use in Southern
Hemisphere.

108

have missed. On one occasion a young mother postponed her birthday celebration in order not to miss a parents' evening.

At the evaluation session, pastors often say:

* People seem to be more interested in matters of faith than we thought.

* People really are interested. They don't come together on seven evenings and for seven celebrations just for nothing. There is a real hunger for guidance among young families and young married couples. The attendance and participation of the parents is really tremendous.

* It convinced me that the co-operation of the faithful at pastoral level is not mere talk.

The invitation

Bearing in mind the aim, and all we have said about it, it would not be fitting either in the letters of invitation or in the first contacts, to begin on a negative note: 'You have problems with your faith . . : You don't know what to do . . . You are bound to have some doubts . . . .' In our opinion this is not a good starting point. It would be better to start: 'You want the best for your child . . . we are offering you an opportunity to help him.'

We should also be careful how the letter is worded. The invitation to participate in this family catechesis does not ask parents to decide at once whether or not their child should make his First Communion. It only asks them to think about whether they, their child, and the rest of their family, would like to move into closer communion with the local christian community or not.

If there is no communication in a family, then we can hardly speak about 'holy communion' of people in Christ with God, because it will have no foundation.

15. THE PARENTS' EVENING

* Why must parents be roped in? Leave things as they were. The school did it adequately.

* The teacher can prepare the children for First Communion much better than we can. She's been trained for it . . . .

* Surely that's why we send our child to a Catholic school? What contribution does the school make now?

* They are just trying to make things easier for themselves, and they expect parents to do their work for them. No thank you!

These are just a few of the remarks we picked up in a parish centre before the first parents' meeting began. Gradually the room filled up. There were about thirty parents altogether. They each received a file. On the cover it read: 'They'll know we are Christians by our love.' In the file were a few pages for the first month, the text, an explanation and further suggestions about what could be done at home.

A short introduction made it clear that there are distinct differences between the task of the school, the task of the parents and the task of the parish in the religious education of the children.

Meditative happening

When the organisational part is over, the real business of equipping parents begins in the form of a reflection. This part is meant to be a truly religious happening. The pastor begins with a prayer or a short reading from scripture using events from daily experience for reflection. He tries to keep as close as possible to the experience of the parents, to restate their questions and worries, and with hope and trust leads them to discover light and joy. This could quite easily take about half-an-hour.

The first parents' evening provides considerable food for thought for a large number of parent-couples. We start with the reality of the family. There we discover a basic form of communication. As believers, we can see it as a fundamental form of our communion in Christ.

We are not concerned with presenting a beautiful meditation on communication. We are working towards practical conclusions on communication: if there is no communication in a family, if the people there do not 'communicate' with each other, then we can scarcely begin to speak about holy communion with Christ in God because it will have no foundation whatsoever. This eternal value cannot become the deepest foundation of their reality, because the reality itself is not present. 'If any one says ''I love God'' and hates his brother, he is a liar; for he who does not love his brother whom he has seen, cannot love God whom he has not seen' (1 John 4:20).

We regularly hear from pastors that they are impressed by the silence and attention of parents during meditation. They are amazed by it. They sense that people are thinking, pondering and discovering together. The wealth which lies behind all the ordinary elements of their lives is evident. This is about their lives.

Not bad at all!

Over a cup of coffee tongues are loosened and you hear remarks like:
* we have known about all these things for a long time, but it is good to realise what a miracle really lies hidden beneath it all . . . .

* it is good to realise that everything we do really springs from our conviction, and from faith . . . .

* of course we do all that, but we have never actually considered that it really meant serving God. So of course we haven't been making that clear to the children . . . .

These comments are different from those overheard at the beginning. You can sense an atmosphere of satisfaction and surprise. Everyone feels that what is happening is concerned with them more than with their children.

'What struck us most,' one parent-couple said later, 'was the willingness of the pastors to think and feel with the parents in the difficulties they have in trying to pass on to their children the things they regard as valuable. There were a lot of trimmings in the past, of course, and it's hard to give them up.'

For the remainder of the evening people talk in groups about what has been said. The task sheets are discussed. These offer practical suggestions for getting ideas across to the child and to the family through short plays, stories and games; there are also ideas on how to be creatively active with the children at home. There is a page of prayers for the home (not children's prayers!) which link up with the meditation for the month. Some plans can be made for a celebration. The evening passes quickly.

Not everything can be solved in one evening — they must come back for more.

Criticism

The first evening does not always run smoothly, nor is its purpose immediately clear to everyone. As one father remarked:

'On November 13 we began family catechesis in our parish. What was it all about? Well that's exactly what we parents were asking ourselves!'

'On the first evening we went along to the parish hall with mixed feelings. Did they want to use this opportunity to talk parents into more religion or more frequent church attendance? (Not such a bad idea, at that). No, they began with a reflection on communication, communicating with one another in one's own family. Talking to each other. But what do you talk about? Playing and having time for each other. Caring for each other, especially in the Christmas season. Pretty soon the criticism was raised: but you do all these things in every normal family anyway. We don't see the point of it; but we talked it over at home, we asked the children. We read the handouts about this family catechesis through again.

'After that came the second evening. Then things fell into

place. We understood: we must do more with our children. Plans were made for organising the Christmas treat. Little assignments were made. At home, questions were being asked. Questions which we as parents had preferred to gloss over. Now there was the opportunity to go into them. Other questions came up, like: What else are we going to do in this communion project? Then came the baptismal ceremony, Lenten observances and Easter. The thing was becoming alive as we progressed.'

Crossing the border-line

We are aware that even the first reflection on communication in the family can arouse strong emotions in a number of those present. This is difficult to avoid. In every group of parents there will be some from broken families, migrant fathers, unmarried mothers, divorced parents, families where a break has occurred with the older children, where people are alienated from each other or who make a life difficult for each other, especially where faith or religion is concerned.

Many a pastor asks himself whether he should refer to the 'home situation' at all. He may be particularly anxious about all the reactions that he triggers off and whether he can handle them. He may be fearful of opening old wounds or uncertain about whether he is really doing the right thing by opening people's eyes. This anxiety can cause him to give up. He can see no good coming from it but rather the opposite.

In our opinion this raises the question of the pastor's own faith in the message of salvation for the future, in spite of all the pain and distress of the past. It touches on the belief that people can cross the boundary from death to life again and again. Not to have any hope is to regard the helpless state in which people find themselves as an unfortunate condition in which little or nothing can be changed, in which they must try to live as best they can, and which they shouldn't be bothered about. After all, you can't change adults!

Humanly speaking, perhaps you can't. But, as a believer, can you seriously think that a particular person is beyond salvation?

We must have grave doubts about a pastoral approach which

sees no point in helping another person get a better insight into the reality of his unwholesome situation: that is a pastoral approach which begins with the idea that there is no hope for a particular person. Can it be called 'pastoral' if somebody listens patiently, gives a pat on the shoulder, and gives routine advice which changes nothing? Tranquillisers and alcohol soften the pain of life a little. But there is no mention of liberation and resurrection. Obviously religion has had its day for these people.

But there can be redemption and salvation in life. We believe this, so we have the right and duty to approach these parents with the holy conviction that this can be a border-line situation for them. Their situation need not be experienced as unhappy and terminal, it also holds a promise of salvation for them. Past events may have been unfortunate but the possibility of active intervention and of change lies before them.

This can lead to improvement and salvation for these people themselves, and to new happy relationships with others concerned. With God's help it is possible to cross this border-line.

It demands courage and conviction, and at the same time the prudence and tact of a true believer to approach marriage and family problems as border-line situations, as moments of decision. It requires expertise, sensitivity and education, but success does not lie so much in the hands of the pastor as in the trust and faith of the people themselves, that with the help of God they will be able to succeed.

This catechesis pleads that border-line situations should be regarded as ones that can be resolved. The causes of the difficulties can be discovered, the challenge to go beyond them by a process of change can be accepted.

A meaningful exchange of views is possible only after parents have had practical experience of the topic for the month at home.

16. WORKING IT OUT IN PRACTICE

The parents' evenings are not meant to be opportunities for holding discussions on just any topic. We know how easily 'discussions' can degenerate into endless arguments where one or two people impose themselves on the whole group.

To enter into discussion on the first evening does not make sense. There is as yet no common basis for meaningful dialogue because parents do not fully understand this type of catechesis. They still have to apply it. Only after they have had a month's practical experience at home do they begin to understand. To exclude the danger of a discussion which may wreck a whole evening, handouts are drawn up for the participants to browse through. These are given out at the beginning of the evening. They serve to get a focussed discussion going by posing a number of questions about hypothetical cases. The questions are drawn up in such a way that parents do not get into a discussion with each other about the theme, but they talk themselves into the theme.

The course of the subsequent evenings is different: the parents can now speak from experience. They have their own little story. They are now ready for conversation with each other. Parents exchange their experiences, support each other in their difficulties or, at least, comfort themselves with the discovery that others do not enjoy instant success either. In this way they are evaluating the proceedings of the past month and commenting on suggestions made in the file.

The parents' evening begins as soon as the first parents arrive. They are met by the members of the work-group and immediately discussions begin in small groups. This has many advantages: people do not have to wait until everybody is there. In a small

115

group they talk more easily about what is on their minds. They get every possible encouragement: they can offer criticisms, make suggestions, exchange experiences, plan things together and carry them out. The danger that the whole meeting could be held up or wrecked by the frustrations of one of the participants is practically ruled out. But the most important thing is this: people can speak about what vitally concerns them. Gradually they learn to express their own faith and doubts.

In this way, the whole project becomes their own. The natural leaders among those present will automatically assume more responsibility and, from among these, 'co-workers' will emerge.

By the time the discussions in small groups have ended, even the latecomers will have arrived! The discussion leader sees that the experiences of the small groups are briefly shared in assembly either then or at a later stage.

Outline of a Parents' Evening

A suggested programme:

Feedback: When parents arrive they are asked:
   — What did you think of the previous evening?
   — What did you think of the celebration?
   — How did things go at home?
People help each other by contributing from their experience. The leader makes a brief summary of everything and leads on to the next stage.

Browsing: With the help of a discussion paper, the subject for the evening is opened up. It is recommended that parent-couples go into different groups.

   Afterwards husband and wife can exchange ideas: 'And what did they say in your group?' 'What did you say?' etc.

Reflection: All the groups then come together and briefly relate their experiences. Then the leader offers a reflection on the theme of the month. In this reflection he sums up the findings of the groups, he tries to show their deeper faith-dimensions and adds further meditative and enriching considerations.

Interval: Tea or coffee.

For the home: At this stage reference is made to the 'feedback' activities for the home, the children's afternoons and the celebrations planned.

If the work-group wishes, the programme can also be arranged as follows:
Browsing, Reflection, Interval, Feedback, and For the Home.

Some random suggestions

*Do not hand out the whole parents' file at once. The file is so arranged that instalments can be added month by month. Parents have then sufficient time to assimilate the material in each instalment with their family, to integrate it and to make it their own. The reflections at the monthly parents' evenings do not deal with what parents should tell their children, but the introductions and themes are so closely linked to the situation in which they live, that they can actually be lived out. The point of departure and, to a large extent, the content is their everyday experience. In this project these are seen primarily in the light of communication in the family.

This awareness awakens such a sense of wonder and joy that parents are automatically inspired to live according to it and to celebrate it.

At home the CHILD enjoys the result of this renewed appreciation of communion in Christ through the experiences of everyday living. Moreover, the child who is preparing First Communion gets special attention. For this reason each instalment of the file contains some 'ideas for the home'.

*The file is not intended for *private use*. Parents should not simply take it home and work out for themselves how to prepare their child. The project aims at the formation of mini-communities made up of several individuals and families, who, for several months, are involved in the same activities. The fundamental idea of communion is considerably broader than communicating only with one's own family or of going to communion in the church with one's parents: it is pre-eminently the celebration of union with each other in the local community of faith.

117

*The celebrations are an essential part of the whole project and are just as important as the parents' evenings. It is usually here that the theme of the month becomes really meaningful for the child. Catechesis becomes visual. Here faith is given liturgical expression, for the parents as well as for the children. Then questions come thick and fast from the child and parents get the chance to clarify things they have been trying to explain during the month. Through these celebrations, generation gaps are bridged and real community-building occurs.

We shall return to the task of the parish in religious education in more detail later.

*It is important to have a good *photographer* present at the celebrations, one who knows how to take good action shots. If these photos are displayed in the church afterwards all the parishioners can get to know about family catechesis. Parents order photos of their own children and put them in the family album. These spark off conversations with family and acquaintances about what they experienced that year in the parish. In this way their own story grows and they perform their christian duty of witnessing and excercising the apostolate without any special effort. Photographs can be called the modern version of the picture bibles of the early cathedrals. These helped the simple folk of the time to relate stories of faith to each other. Similarly, photographs help today's parents to relate what they have experienced as high points in the living of their faith with their children.

*To begin a family catechesis project three months before Christmas does not, at first sight, seem opportune; but it is important as an introductory *period* for group formation, for building up a positive attitude and for creating an optimal foundation for the more explicit catechesis of the sacraments later on. In fact this part, which has a climax in the feast of Christmas, always succeeds and this motivates parents.

N.B. In the diagram on pp. 120-1 we give a synopsis of the communion-project. Each column gives the outlines of the theme for the month: of the human experiences from which to begin, how these are interpreted in faith, what possibilities there are for the believing community, and the role of the school.

OUTLINE OF COMMUNION-PROJECT
(According to the Liturgical Year)

OUR FAMILY
(first reflection)

Our family is a basic model of communication. The Christian family is the basic model of Holy Communion. It is the heart of the believing community, of all God's family.
FAMILY MASS

CHILD IN THE HOME
(second reflection)

A child in the home is enriched and made happy by all who share its family life. When the child is introduced into the believing community he experiences the bond that unites him with all who are at home in God's family.
CHRISTMAS CELEBRATION

SET ON THE WAY
(third reflection)

The child can now journey with all the people who are making their way to God. Baptism sets the child on his way. The child learns to draw strength from him who is the Way, the Truth and the Life.
CELEBRATION OF BAPTISM

LIFE AND DEATH
(fourth reflection)

Christ is the way of Life. To follow his way means: being able to give up things; again and again to leave something behind in order to move on; to let go; to make sacrifices; to die in order to live.
LENTEN CAMPAIGN

HEALTHY LIFE
(fifth reflection)

It is always hard to let go of certain things — and not to become possessed by objects to the extent that we sacrifice people for them. The Lamb of God can free us from such obsession and heal us.
PENITENTIAL SERVICE

ETERNAL LIFE
(sixth reflection)

Through our communion with Christ, he himself becomes our food. He gives us the strength to continue on the road to God, because he is both spiritual food and eternal life.
FIRST COMMUNION

	I OUR FAMILY (October)	II CHILD IN THE HOME (November)	III SET ON THE WAY (January)
Human Experience	The family is the basic model of communication — the heart of society — mutual: giving-receiving — makes life possible, pleasant, happy — gives purpose to life, to each other, to the child	The child is both gift and challenge to its parents — likewise parents are gift and challenge to their child — entrusted to or at each other's mercy — mystery of passing on life; birth — living off and for each other gift of love in daily bread — rich in each other; grateful	Birth: the ways of people — becoming human through each other — learning to live in the spirit of a nation, language, laws But: inherited attitude of WE! and THEY! — cause of division, sin, war
Believing Experience	COMMUNION The Christian family is the basic model of Holy Communion — heart of the believing community, of the whole family of God, the whole of mankind Choice of leading children into this community of faith, to let them communicate in Christ.	THE FATHER'S HOUSE Being a child of the Father; rich and happy with everyone; grateful for all that is good. Life is a gift of God: child of God. Good tidings. Father — religion, authority, Christmas. God's Son. Praying to God.	PEOPLE OF GOD Baptism: the way of God — together journeying on with all others in the spirit of God. — Drawing strength from the source of living water. Religion of brotherhood, love of neighbour. — Liberation from Original Sin, Ten Commandments, law of love.
At Home	Children learn more from experience than explanations. Co-operation in ordinary things; telling stories, reading aloud, party games, (father included) We belong together: Who?	Gift and response, expectation and surprise (Santa Claus). Christmas story and crib. Togetherness and conviviality. Christmas dinner. The guest at the table. Advent practices	All people, cultures, all are different. Therefore rules, customs, law of all peoples differ. Water is source of life, through the waters of Baptism a divine life. Together on the way.
Parish	FAMILY MASS OR WEDDING Long-term pastoral plan: work-group of parents pastoral co-workers catechetical songs.	CHRISTMAS CELEBRATION Advent practices: break and share. Showing children around church and home. Catechetical songs of Christmas.	BAPTISMAL CELEBRATION Unity of Christians, — ecumenism, universal, church. — diocese, church community, parish council. Catechetical songs about water and being on the way.
School	Communication is a basic element in the syllabus of the early primary school years. Call parents together about this central theme — model of parent-movement.	Learning to make surprise-packets, Christmas decorations, cards, Christmas play or celebration, expectation and peace.	Origin of our nation in struggle and perseverance. All different: laws? slides (the story of the drop of water).

	IV LIFE & DEATH (February)	V HEALTHY LIFE (March)	VI ETERNAL LIFE (April)
Human Experience	Nature: living and dying: Society: buying. People: consume each other, pass on life. Growth: child "dies" to become an adolescent — adult. — leaving things behind in order to move on. — well-being above welfare. — doing justice.	Health is the greatest possession: physical-spiritual unity. Disease of our culture: means before people — poor substitutes in education — obsession which becomes mute or aggressive — ready for doctor, psychiatrist or priest?	Law of life and living by and for each other. Love is: giving oneself as food for others. — human depth of life eating from each other — bread is more than mere food.
Believing Experience	SACRIFICE Mortification — dying in order to live, way of life: I am the Way, the Life not standing still, holding on, but letting go, leaving behind (sacrifice) to go further (happiness). Losing oneself for the sake of others and thus finding oneself.	LAMB OF GOD Healing and liberation, redemption. — standing still, holding on, is sin — putting things before people, obsession, isolation. The Lamb of God takes away sins, require faith and the will to let go. Healthy faith.	THE MEAL Food for eternal life to be able to go further along the way of God. Love is: giving one's life as food for others. Fulfilment of law of life: eternal life, eating at source of life: mystery of our faith: Christ our food.
At Home	Living in nature: spring cycle, recurring cycle. Fasting for health for others Lenten campaign — appreciating food and drink — learning use of money — devoting time to others.	Living healthily is living in faith, keeping an open mind. Hands: receiving, giving; "besetting sin" recognisable by its results: muteness, aggression. Liberation from egoism through Christ to others. Penance — healing clearing up	At meals life is handed on, experience of unity in living. — family customs — feast of the whole family — inviting guests Prepare gifts for fellow parishioners and visiting them — breaking and sharing.
Parish	LENTEN PRACTICES Continue with theme of water: — drink for life and growth water-wine — people in need (desert) giving to drink Catechetical songs about seed, bread.	PENITENTIAL SERVICE Unmasking and liberation, water, purifying, healing against pollution, the Flood, John the Baptist, reparation, penance. Catechetical songs. Palm Sunday, be converted.	EUCHARIST Practice, prepare. Addresses of parishioners for visiting, gifts. Exhibition of scrap-book, family catechesis photos. Water: small gifts like drop of water in the chalice.
School	Grain of wheat. New life in nature; visit to zoo, aquarium, farm.	Catechetical project on the prodigal son. Pottery: hands Make masks for celebration. Easter.	For all children and parents: Day of Communication Make decorations for the feast in church: group work (altar hanging)

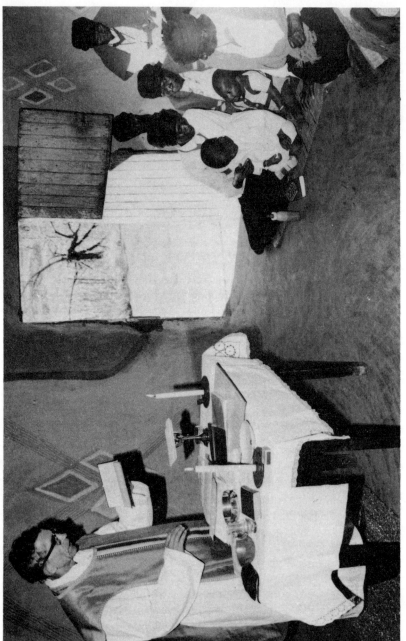

*You may think you know
what you are starting when
you join in family catechesis,
but you don't really know
what you are letting yourself
in for. It is not a question
of having time, but of
fixing priorities.*

17. INTERNAL DIVISION OF TASKS

Pastors as well as lay people realise after a time that they haven't just begun a communion-project but that they have entered into a process. It brings each one face to face with a number of questions and problems. It is a challenge and those who think that they can manage on their own may find they have bitten off more than they can chew. Team-work is absolutely essential.

The pastors

'Being the Church' means working together. This applies to pastors as well. We regard it of fundamental importance that the pastors who are doing the same project should meet monthly in groups of six or eight to evaluate their activities and experiences and to prepare for the coming month. This provides support, encouragement, confirmation and often comfort and patience, through hearing how things are going with others. We have already seen on occasion that many pastors anxiously ask themselves if they are really able to cope with what they have awakened in people. One pastor on his own will find it difficult to meet the demands entailed. This requires skilful guidance and for many, special training. Taking counsel together has a formative and inspiring effect and creates team spirit among neighbouring pastors. These are all important things and ways of doing them are best sought together.

The positive side of these *gatherings* is not that they become general talking sessions, but that they are planned work-sessions where pastoral problems are given priority. Many meetings of this kind are theoretical and non-committal. The gatherings we have in mind deal with matters which concern each participant. If they are led by someone from a deanery or from a catechetical centre, much more comes of them and everyone is able to benefit.

* The *reflections* in the file are purposely not worked out in great detail. They give only the main outline of the thought, in short phrases. The intention is that each leader should make these basic ideas his own and turn them into a personal meditatiion. It would be a good idea to stencil the meditation and distribute it to the parents with the monthly sheets for the home.

* As soon as possible each pastor should try to form a *work-group* selected from the parish council, the parent-teachers' association of the school, a teacher, creative young people from the colleges or the youth choir, and a few of the parents concerned. In the long run pastoral co-workers will emerge from this group, and they will be indispensable to see things through.

Without a work-group the goals, viz. building up a laity-centred church, laity formation and lay leadership will not be realised and all the efforts will just peter out every year.

Tasks

For the work-group and, later on, for the pastoral co-workers a large number of tasks needs to be undertaken.

1 *The preparation*
* go through the parish and school card file to find the families who qualify for this project;

* send out invitations to the parents to participate;

* make contact with the Catholic schools and Parent-Teachers' Associations and get their co-operation;

* make special provision for extra help for parents of children at non-Catholic schools, and for the children themselves;

* establish contact by phoning or visiting parents who do not reply to the printed circulars;

* it is recommended that those who say, 'We are not taking part' or who do not respond be tactfully asked why. Often there is some inadequate objection and the obstacle which holds them back can easily be removed. For example: 'We have just recently come to live here . . . we do not know anyone.' After a conversation you can say: 'You will be there that evening, won't you . . . .' 'Yes, you can rely on me to be there.'

    We have also heard such remarks as: 'We are not taking part because the thing is entirely in the hands of the laity!' The work-group had forgotten to include the name of the priest among the names of the organising committee.

* arrange publicity in the parish newsletter

* in general, see to typing and stencilling

* if possible, send out or deliver in advance the introduction from the parents' file

* organise a baby-sitting service.

2 *The beginning*
* Prepare the first parents' evening for October (or May).

* If the project can be started even earlier, it is a good idea to devote one evening to a study of the new approach and to invite all interested parties: parents, principals, teachers and catechists. This can prevent much frustration at subsequent evenings and can save much time.

* For the sake of clarity, it is recommended that the meetings with parents should not be held on school premises but in the parish hall, the presbytery or elsewhere so that it is clear that this offer stems from the parish.

* Prepare the hall to make the whole thing look pleasant, make all the necessary arrangements.

* On the parents' evening, welcome the parents and introduce them to one another.

* Keep a record of attendance.

N.B. Keeping a record of attendance is important. Then the work group will know who attended and who did not. Then they have an opportunity to take the notes to those parents who were absent and to go through them (provided there is no other problem). Usually there is a reason for absence and a helping hand can be extended by the worker himself or the matter can be referred to the pastor. This leads to purposeful home-visiting.

Suggestion: Have name tags ready for each person at the entrance.
* This makes it possible for people to address each other by name.

* It is a quick way of helping people to get to know each other (having a name in a group is an important factor in belonging in the church)

* Moreover one can unobtrusively check who is absent.

Alternative plan for first evening
Because it sometimes happens that some parents come to a first evening in a critical frame of mind, the following plan can be followed. But care must be taken to keep things under control.

* Allow an hour for people to get rid of all the aggression that they may want to express, let them talk it out; do not challenge their arguments or be on the defensive, accept these people with their feelings of confusion.

* Then invite them to join in the process (with Christmas as a goal for a start).

* In this way, lead the discussion away from their problems, their worries, their emotionalism and negativism and towards a more positive attitude by means of an indirect pastoral offer: an offer which concerns their child.

3 Leading the discussion
It can be very stimulating if the pastor plans the discussion paper with the work-group beforehand. This gives the co-workers a somewhat firmer footing. They will join in a group of parents more confidently and be of assistance when discussion does not get going easily.

The work-group also draws up the questions for the feedback. It is wise to make clear from the first meeting that in group discussions we were not concerned about who is right or who is wrong. On the first evening 'browsing' can be introduced, as follows:

"It is not our intention to *argue* but to listen to each other . . . Each one of us experiences reality in his own way . . . By listening to each other, we get to know and appreciate each other in spite of the fact that we do not think the same . . . Only then is communication possible . . . ."

Communication is: 'Let us have your views?'
'How do you see this?'
'That's interesting. I've never thought of it that way'
'Carry on with what you are saying'
'May I ask . . .'
'What you were saying is very interesting'

Communication is not: 'It is!' or 'It is not' ending with 'Let's not discuss it any further'.

We have much in common: we complement each other!

We all go away richer than when we came. We set each other thinking. By comparing our own opinions with those of others we become more conscious of how we think ourselves . . .

This is surely *meaningful* in a family.

This is the *meaning* of family catechesis.

It is an activity-meeting for parents. It will be practice for what they will be doing at home, especially with the older children.

Thereafter the most important task of the discussion-leaders will be to ensure that people exchange ideas with each other.

Alternative plan for successive evenings

Instead of sending a short reminder for the next parents' evening (reminders are important, and cannot be dispensed with), the next instalment from the file can be sent for preview at home. Then it is useful to enclose a few pertinent questions.

At the parents' evening itself, instead of a reflection one can hold a religious dialogue. During this, people do not so much discuss as question and give testimony together, so that the pastor and the members of the work-group can make their personal contributions.

In cases where the work-group no longer think that the pastor should lead the reflections, but cannot find a person capable of doing it among themselves, then this alternative is an excellent possibility.

4 *Forming groups*

From the second month, the parents can gather in small groups (which include one or two people from the work-group). They can exchange experiences with each other. Parents are eager to speak about what they have discovered, to mention what is going well, and give vent to what frustrates them.

They need somebody to listen, to keep the discussion in order, and to give everyone a chance to have his say. As time goes on people will begin to explain themselves, to question and to witness to each other. This is where the real interaction takes place. When all the parents have finally arrived, the most important points which have come up in each group are summarised and shared with the larger group.

This joint discussion serves as an evaluation of the previous month and of the project as a whole.

On the first evening, the parents still talk of 'they'. 'They' must do this, why don't 'they' do that? As long as this goes on, they are setting themselves over against those who organise. They expect the organisers to spoon-feed them, to do everything for them. They criticise and continue to complain that the teacher at school can do it much better. They must be helped to switch over to 'WE' as quickly as possible. To succeed in this:

* At every proposal say: 'Who will tackle this'

* Do not consider that every question or criticism is directed at you, or that you ought to answer it personally. Refer it to the group, thereby involving everybody.

* Ask for the help and the co-operation of the parents in everything that has to be done.

* However good the liturgy group or 'creative club' may be it is always 'better' if the parents have done it themselves.

* Let them arrange their own activities as far as possible. The work-group can of course help a little.

5 *The children's scrapbook*

* From the first evening encourage parents to start a scrapbook with their child. This can include drawings, task sheets, photos of family events, texts of the family masses or celebrations, the text of the Christmas story, the crib figures that were made, the child's baptismal certificate, etc.

* To give parents an idea of how to do this and to inspire them to carry out the tasks have part of a scrapbook ready yourself (let your children make it for you!)

* Show parents how the various tasks can be carried out — surprise gifts made, Christmas cards designed etc.

* Now and again let parents bring the scrapbook to the celebrations and include it in the liturgy.

6 *Parish catechesis directed to children*

The resource file includes suggestions 'FOR SCHOOL OR PARISH'. There are many schools where more than half the children no longer participate in church life. Other children are not at Catholic schools. Therefore these suggestions 'for school or parish' can be used for catechetical afternoons with the children (and parents) in the parish.

* These meetings can also be used for working together on the more difficult tasks suggested. In which case, these tasks should not be distributed on the parents' evening but should be reserved for the children's afternoons. This is a good opportunity for the children to bring their scrapbooks with them and to work on them together.

* It is quite easy to practise the hymns for the next celebration of the month with the children. At the same time these can be explained, and afterwards illustrated, dramatised or danced.

* The liturgy or celebration of the month can also be prepared and practised at these parish-catechesis afternoons. Be sure to involve the parents here too.

7 *Follow-up*

When we tell the people in October (May) that we intend to hold six parents' evenings, there are always a number who look very doubtful: Why so many? Yet when the six evenings plus four or five celebrations are over, the common reaction is: Yes, but you can't just leave us now! We must carry on. Isn't there anything more for the children and for us? This reaction comes as a surprise.

Many pastors start thinking in terms of a Bible course for this group or a sort of continuation course or adult catechesis. Many participants want this kind of pastoral care but they can fall back into the old consumer attitude, demanding too much of the pastor's attention and tying him to their small group. He could keep that up for another two years, but what then?

It is much better to close off the communion-project at its climax in the celebration of communion. The mini-community can then peacefully disband. Because the whole process takes place within the parish, we won't necessarily lose these people. They can orientate themselves anew of their own accord and join another existing group in the parish.

Many pastors hold an evaluation evening. It is a good idea to give people an overall view of the different groups and activities in the parish liturgy, teaching and community life. The contact addresses should be listed, and application forms filled in on the spot. A number of follow-up parish catechetical activities such as a parallel children's service, family masses, can also be suggested and people can be invited to participate in them.

*If you want to belong to a
community, then there are
two essential conditions:
you must be personally
present and you must join in.*

18. PROJECT AND PROCESS

(See Table II p. 132)

The family catechesis of the First Communion-project has been
favourably received. If we ask what the first effective result of the
project is, then the answer will be that it gives content to a process
which affects not just a few individuals but all concerned. It
creates community. The church really happens there. In order to
form a community two things are of fundamental importance.
They are essential requirements:
* physical presence, a meeting with each other. You cannot
  make a community with 'I belong, but I don't come'.

* a joint project: something you are involved in together, where
  you can exchange views and which fulfils a need. Something
  for which people work and struggle together always brings
  them together.

First phase: family catechists

The project gathers all together and gives them something on
which to focus. It works as an inspiration and people grow towards
each other.
  This brings about a two-fold growth for each one personally:
a movement inwards, through the interaction of the group, by
which each one gradually becomes more fully himself; and a
movement outwards, in the functioning of each one through his
task in the family, the neighbourhood, the job, in his own place.
By means of such a project, the *pastor* attains the clarification of
his function. His task is to inspire, to stimulate, to assist; he is

131

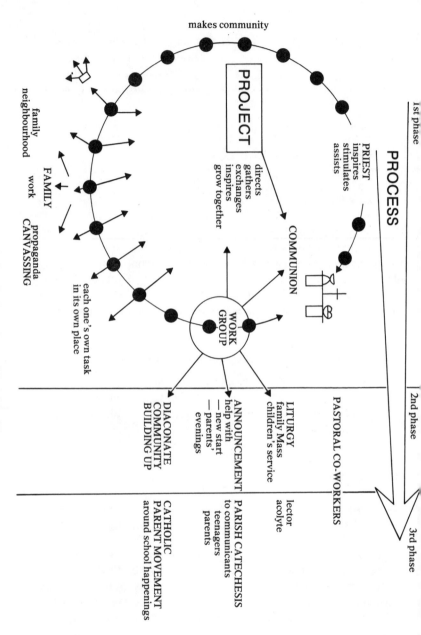

Table II: Family Catechesis as a Pastoral Project and Process

a participant, guiding and being of service and no longer dominating or having to carry the sole responsibility and do the job practically all on his own.

If he still has to do everything himself, then he has made mistakes in his attitude to parents. Clear signs of this are: a continuous fall in the number of participants and the persistent tendency to hand back responsibility to the professional.

Where the project has really become the concern of the whole group, he acts as animator for *family catechists*, because it makes catechists of all the participants.

Among them there will always be motivated people who offer to help where they can. From among these a work-group will emerge spontaneously. They will work with the pastor to ensure the smooth running of the project itself, by giving assistance to parents and by preparing, arranging and organising all manner of things.

With this the project sparks off a process which works fruitfully for the participants within the group, and also makes each one helpful to those whom they touch by their activities, firing them with their enthusiasm.

Among believers, this communication process demands to be celebrated in the holy *communion* of all in Christ. This celebration becomes truly a sacramental sign of a reality which signifies the spiritual riches already abundantly present. It gives to each one personally, and to all together, a new enrichment in their spiritual lives.

Second phase: pastoral co-workers

When the goal of the project has been reached, most people do not want to stop. The inspiring and gathering function of the project is now taken over by the process which has been set in motion. This leads to a second phase in which the work-group and other motivated people assume a new and more significant role. Now the pastor finds himself surrounded by true pastoral co-workers.

By this we mean parishioners who take their right and duty of evangelisation seriously and who therefore offer their services in the community of faith, especially in the religious education of the youth of the parish.

A primary task for these pastoral co-workers is to help initiate the next group of parents and children into the communion-project.

Other possibilities are:

* the formation by these parents of a movement focussed on the total education of their children.

* the independent organising of family catechesis by a number of parent couples and their children in their own homes.

* involvement in the Confirmation project, and especially teenage catechesis.

* an on-going family catechesis for parents with children at state secondary schools.

Third phase: leadership training

These pastoral co-workers will require special guidance from the pastor. This will involve him in extra work but eventually they will take much work off his hands. Only in this way can we ensure the building up of the church of the laity, where more and more of the faithful dare to be and want to be 'their brother's keeper'. The pastor must give priority to this over all kinds of traditicnal service which the people will continue to demand of him as passive objects of his pastoral care.

Pastoral responsibility of each believer

Besides the official names of priest and pastoral worker, we have introduced into 'family catechesis' the term 'pastoral co-worker'. From of old the term *pastoral* has had a technical meaning and suggests care of souls by office-bearers — the particular task of the pastor, the professional. We want to understand it in the wider sense without, however, leaving out the notion of 'professional contribution' of the office-bearer. Under 'pastoral' we wish to understand first of all:

The Christian attitude of being-your-brother's-keeper

By this we do not mean guardianship. What we do mean is part of the art of living and the ability to give others room to grow: paying attention to their life problems and feelings and contributing to a climate in which people feel that they are not isolated.

The Christian is stimulated by the belief that God's name means: I-am-here-for-you and through you I am here for others. He wants people to have room to grow and to realise that he does not abandon them in any life situation, not even in death.

It is the task of faith to bring home to people this confidence and these good tidings, especially when they are seeking for meaning and courage in the midst of life's problems (problems that may be external, or ones they make for themselves). Mgr Ernst, Bishop of Breda, once said: 'Where faith becomes work in the service of the faith of others, then I speak of *pastoral work*.'

We would like to call this work a vital function of a community of faith and insist on describing it as *pastoral*. One could speak of 'Christian life style' or of 'mission' and reserve the word 'pastoral' for the professional pastors.

The *disadvantage* of this is that the majority of the faithful go on seeing themselves as passive recipients of a pastoral care which is exercised by a few.

But where believers themselves, in the midst of society, in their own way place their faith at the service of others, what they are doing is pastoral work even if it is not explicitly professional.

We need to use the *term* pastoral in order to reduce the gap between what people are capable of and the image they have of pastoral work.

'Professional pastors' will have to direct their efforts towards making believers aware of their responsibility and stimulating them to exercise pastoral care of others. This will require practice and guidance for pastors themselves and for all the faithful: they will need skills in communicating with people, regular reflection to deepen their own sense of mission and continuous attention to the good news.

This guidance can be provided by a pastor who has been released for this particular task. His aim will be the building up of a church in which more and more believers become 'their brother's keeper'.

Pastoral care should be exercised by many people because it is many faceted.

We will not solve the problem of ministry in the church just by ordaining deacons or mature married men. Nor will this kind of ordinand be found except in the ranks of those who in their 'lay' life have experienced what 'pastoral functioning' is.

Training is not the first essential. What is important is a practical and conscious experience of one's own dealings in faith with others. Only then is it understandable that some believers should become more proficient and receive from the church an official charge to go out and make others aware of their pastoral possibilities.

Unless the faithful experience for themselves that it is worthwhile to devote some of their time and skills to pastoral work, the church will no longer be able to count on leaders who want to make it their life's work.

The concept of pastoral work must be widened beyond the confines of the 'professional'.

PART IV
EDUCATORS IN THE FAITH

The assumption that faith is, above all, a matter of knowing, is the most persistent misconception with which we have to contend at present. Knowledge and science are the latest idol-images in which our faith has been cast.

* Parents do not have to *'play school'* at home. That is not the intention. Religious education is concerned in the first place with one's own personal attitude and one's living of the faith. In comparison to this, religious knowledge is just secondary (p. 142).

* Family catechesis works on the principle *'first practise, then talk'*. This is in direct contrast to the school method 'first know, then do',. a method which is still most highly rated (p. 146).

* The first *'milieu of faith'* is the family. Parents are the primary educators of their children. Faith and religion are not the same thing. Faith happens in the living relations between people, and in relationships with God, here and now. Religion can become a mannerism and an outward show. Religious education in the family is the most important dimension of family life from the cradle to the grave (p. 149).

* The second *'milieu of faith'* is the believing community of faith. The community has its own particular task in the religious education of youth. Concern for youth is growing in more and more parishes. Children must play an important part in the liturgy, for they are the future of the church (p. 156).

* The biggest stumbling block for children at present is the *Sunday liturgy*. Children do not seem to belong there. They show by their behaviour that there is something quite fundamentally wrong with our liturgy. It is on the whole no longer a celebration of an intensely lived mystery of faith (p. 159).

* There must always be *interaction* between the experience of faith at home and the religious celebration in church. A liturgical celebration happens in a vacuum unless there has already been some related preparatory activity in the family beforehand. Hopefully, children are helping us to find the way to a real liturgical renewal (p. 165).

* Finally, the diagram which follows sketches what we think are the possibilities for co-operation in *team work* and *task sharing* among family, parish and school (p. 170).

    In this field the church still has enormous work to do.

*Many parents cannot get
away from the idea that
they are supposed to start
'playing school'. Some
simply do not want to 'play
school' and make difficulties.
Others did try and found
that it failed.*

19. NOT 'PLAYING SCHOOL'

'When the teacher or the priest says something, it makes a far
deeper impression on the children than when we do. We have
not been trained for this. I certainly have no intention of playing
school at home or of passing on my own doubts to my children.'

Time and again this crops up: 'If I do it myself, will my child
really know all the facts? Will he really understand who he is
receiving in the sacred host?' (Do you really understand it yourself?) 'Have I told my daughter everything correctly?'

Here we are dealing with a misconception. Many parents
think that they must be able to talk well about these things to
their children; that they must be able to explain everything
in the finest detail if the children are to understand it. Most of
them think that they must play school at home. Naturally they
have never acted like school-teachers and have no intention
of doing so. Only now that preparation for First Communion
is at hand do they try to do so. And this is exactly what must
not happen.

It is amazing that children just won't take it either. 'They
found it a nuisance. Sometimes it was difficult to get the child
interested.'

We heard similar comments from many parents. Quite jokingly
one mother told of her experience. 'I sat down with my child at
the table. I could not find the right words. I did not know what to
say. Then I had to go and do something in the kitchen. My little
girl followed me. While I was busy, the words came spontaneously.'

That is exactly the way it happens at home. You do not solemnly sit down opposite the child if you want to say or discuss something. In that way you become tongue-tied. No, it happens spontaneously. If in fact preparation for First Communion consisted chiefly in explanations and expositions, in a lot of talking, learning and knowing, then clearly it would be a task for the teacher or for someone especially trained for the job like the priest. Who would ever dream of giving that responsibility to parents?

Yet the misconception is widespread. Parents think they are now being forced to do something that is really the task of the teachers and the school. This idea is so ingrained in the minds of young and old, rich and poor, educated and uneducated, that we think it is important to consider where it has come from.

If parents think this is what is happening, it is quite understandable if they object and refer the matter back to the school. As long as they persist in this they cannot be clear about the contribution they can make. Yet this contribution is specifically theirs and cannot be taken over by the school.

Assumptions

What first strikes us in examining the causes of this misconception is that parents still think in terms of outmoded assumptions about their children and about our lives and our tasks as adult believers in relation to children. These assumptions stem from the life pattern of twenty years ago or more. They have of course noticed that education has changed, but they have not yet revised their own assumptions. To a large extent this explains the origin of their objections. The most common difficulties are: a one-way traffic in education, the omniscience of authority, and the Catholic faith as a matter of learning and knowing.

1. The idea which many grown-ups have of their relationship to children still reflects a one-way-traffic approach. This is the assumption in all they say and do: We know it all — we have arrived — the child isn't anywhere yet — he still has everything to learn, so we must educate the child. We must pass on what we already have. This attitude is fairly general. There is no sign of reciprocity in the relationship: that children can also educate their parents, that parents can learn from their children, that they are entrusted to each other and are at each

other's mercy. Yet to us this seems fundamental, certainly when it is a matter of the faith-dimension of this parent-child relationship. It is one of the pillars on which our family catechesis is built.

2. In matters of faith and religion it becomes clear that many parents try to cover up their own uncertainty by adopting the 'omniscience-of-authority' attitude.

As adults they are supposed to know everything. And if they don't, they can hardly let it show, certainly not to the children. If they allow that to happen then the children will no longer do what they tell them. Many parents think that they don't count any more.

These parents realise that they are no longer up to date. They have not been able to keep up with it all. To avoid having to admit this, many declare that they are not interested, anyhow. Perhaps in the long run, they even start to believe this themselves for a while.

Now they are told in no uncertain terms that they are responsible for the religious education of their own children. At the same time they are deprived of the possibility of handing it over to the school. They begin to get worried.

It usually begins like this: 'We know all about *it*. We are all for *it*. But how do you *tell* it to your children these days?'

But the real question is: What is *it!* If parents know what to do about this 'it', — their own faith, then it will gradually come across to their children.

3. However, in the question — how to *tell* it, a further assumption is often involved, which prevents ordinary people, but also the more educated ones, from having a clear insight into the religious education of their children. Nowadays you need a solid training for everything and you need to know quite a lot. These days they are convinced that you can only be a good Christian if you *know* enough about it. That is why it so much depends on the school whether their children will be good Catholics later on. That is where they must teach the children the catechism, Bible history, the sacraments, just as we were taught. But nowadays children don't learn anything at school anymore. They don't know anything anymore. 'We were never trained for this. We could never explain that properly to the children.

And the teacher, the master, the priest and the catechist do much too little about it at school. Just what is to become of the religious education of our children?'

These opinions are heard at practically every parents' evening, at every home visit, whenever the question of the religious education of young people crops up. It seems that these people are defending the holiest things, orthodoxy, the heritage of our fathers, but in fact they are fussing about accidentals and forgetting essentials — what it is really about. Or rather, they no longer have any idea or grasp of the fact that, as far as God is concerned, what counts first and foremost is our attitude of faith and that, in comparison, religious knowledge is only secondary.

Yet we are stuck with it

This last assumption, that faith should be chiefly a question of knowledge is, in fact, the most persistent misconception that we come up against. It runs through everything: at home, in church and at school. Knowledge and science are the latest idol-images in which our faith is cast. And they are the exact opposite of the living reality which we have in mind when we speak of belief.

This faith is quite different from the presentation of formulas which can be learnt, which must be known, the knowledge of truths which you must believe because you cannot understand them and cannot see them; saying yes to information guaranteed by God; saying yes to dogmas.

For us faith is looking with different eyes, seeing the mystery in everything, experiencing depth in contact with everyone and every thing, meeting God in the present moment.

As long as this distinction is not clear to parents, they cannot follow us. They are bound to misunderstand us all the time. We can see why they wish to fall back on the school because they find that we do not offer what they expect and what, in their opinion, is most important.

It is obvious that they will not make much of the task which we have ascribed to them as the primary religious educators of their children and that this cannot give them much satisfaction.

A person learns more by
experience than by
explanation.

20. ACT FIRST, THEN TALK

Communication is a mystery of life with which everyone is occupied every day. One learns it best by doing, living and experiencing.

This is precisely the way a child learns at home — he learns automatically by doing things, joining in with his parents and others. As the parents believe so does the child. The family is therefore the best environment in which to learn to associate with one another, the first milieu in which to 'learn to communicate'. In general one learns more by experience than by explanation, especially where the mysteries of life are concerned. In fact these can never be 'explained'. They must be gone through. Then a person becomes inwardly fulfilled. But no one can explain precisely what this fulfilment means. A person who has not been through it, cannot talk about it. To him it is mere fantasy.

Have we ever noticed how strikingly we bear witness to this in the church, especially directly after the consecration?

'When we eat this bread and drink this cup we proclaim . . . .' by doing this, by taking part, we proclaim these mysteries and we bear witness to our faith in them; not by explaining them in fine detail to each other and to the children.

We see this as an indication of the direction we must take when we equip parents for religious education in their families. We must direct their efforts toward living and experiencing, rather than explaining; towards practising rather than theorising and discussing.

Method

The school method which is still held in high esteem begins by explaining in detail, proving, expounding. The verbal-theoretical approach in school seems much more important than practical formation. Practice will come in due time. You are learning for later. You have the rest of your life to put it into practice, they say.

First know, then do! You may object, and suggest that faith is a matter not of knowing but of being; of being a believer in all your actions and omissions. To this you get the answer: Precisely, but you must first know something about it and nowadays children don't know anything at all . . . And there we are stuck in the old groove. Yet all of us have done our level best, through sermons, courses, parents' evenings, guidance and publicity to explain to people the distinction between faith and knowing something about the faith.

In family catechesis we deliberately take another path. We see no point in fighting this misconception with its own weapons: theory, exposition, explanation, discussion. This only makes us all exhausted. And it is counter-productive. It leads to polarisation. Or people imagine that it is still a matter of knowing and learning; but now a new kind of knowing, a new theory. This new sort of knowing is good and the earlier sort is no good any more!

What is the alternative

We feel inclined, at least at the beginning, to avoid all discussion and to dodge all polemic. We promise to deal with these questions later, but first we invite parents to join in and to try out a few things at home with their children, for example to experience communication, and to prepare the Christmas celebration together. We hope by this to lead them to a number of new, positive experiences through which they will themselves sample the difference between doing and knowing, and afterwards we are glad to exchange ideas about their experiences.

We are quite deliberately using the method: *act first, then talk.* It is like learning to swim. First we try to get people into the water. Then they themselves will ask what they must do in order to be able to swim. In fact they are now posing the vital question and they recognise when they get helpful answers. Their confidence grows, and in this way they learn better and more quickly.

Pastors and parents do not usually realise what they are letting themselves in for, certainly not at the beginning. By the time they realise what they have started and the real questions begin to emerge, most of them, fortunately, are so much at home in the situation that they don't withdraw but are willing to go on, further in.

It gives people an opportunity to discuss experiences which they have had, of finding words for what they believe and for what is happening to them. In this way new theories come within their reach and are eagerly taken up or, if not to the point, are dropped. Believers have always done this, but now they begin to see the value of their own experience as a tool for separating the wheat from the chaff.

We consider that we are in good company with this approach.

In the Gospels we read that Jesus began to act first and only afterwards to teach. Act first, and then at least you have something to talk about.

*Parents are the first religious
educators of their children.
If they cannot keep the flame
of faith alive in their own
family then the light will
grow dim.*

21. THE FIRST MILIEU OF FAITH

It is to be hoped that nobody will take it amiss if we say, at the
outset, that we see no point in crossing swords with parents over
the usual controversial issues. Most people will accept this as long
as it does not mean that we just muddle along. There must be
some clarity about what we are trying to do, what we are aiming
at, what our vision is, in short, what the theory is behind this
practical method. It is all very well to ask people at the beginning
to have confidence in us, but on what is this confidence to be
based? This book may be an indication that we have a number of
things clearly in mind. At the same time we can assume that this
book is the outcome of what has become clearer to us during the
past five years of family catechesis.

This book is, however, beyond the reach of most parents. But
in the interests of parents and those who guide them it seemed
a good idea to put together a number of the insights we have
gained so as to share with parents, once they develop a feeling
for what is taking place. If the aim of this process is not "playing
school" and teaching all kinds of things, what is it? What are the
characteristics of a real life of faith in the family and a real religious
education for children?

Faith and religion

We would like to emphasise from the outset that the whole project
is concerned with the life of faith of adults and of their children.
Whatever we do in the field of religion, whatever we prepare or
celebrate, inside or outside the church, is all about the life of faith.

This is obvious, but one cannot stress it too much. The living reality and the child are repeatedly forgotten, because of secondary things which seem to be so necessary. In discussions with parents about their role, we distinguish between faith and religion. Admittedly, if everything is all right, the two continually affect each other, they constantly intertwine. But people often confuse them. Their faith becomes mixed up with religious trimmings, and in certain circles, becomes surrounded by quasi-scientific jargon. Therefore we separate faith and religion, place them side by side, or even in contrast to each other. In this way we are hoping to clarify what we are aiming at. The life of faith then, is the personal relationship of people with each other and with God, the here and now living out of values.*

We are taking *religion* here in its extreme sense — that is what people have made of their faith over the centuries and as it can be seen now in terms of forms and rules when people come together on Sundays. Understood in this way we are dealing with objective expressions. This requires knowledge, special training and expertise.

Faith is something which precedes this and gives content to it. Religion pre-supposes faith. From parents we do not primarily expect education in religion, but education in faith.

Faith is not something reserved only for the church. It is not just a portion of our human condition good only for Sundays or a couple of minutes every day, separate from our work, our TV watching, our sleep or our going to school. It is not a sauce for the pudding. Religion can be merely something we do, a veneer, an outward show. But faith is leaven. It penetrates all our actions. It is our way of life.

To deal with faith is to deal with oneself, how one thinks, lives, acts, judges, and why we do what we do. We try to help people to experience this faith as a dimension of their lives. Out of the abundance of the heart the mouth speaks. This applies to everyone. We do not have to study for this. We speak about it automatically, and not only with our mouth. It speaks through all our actions and omissions. What we do and don't do has a reason, a deeper foundation.

Living is always living in a particular manner according to a specific conviction, according to value judgements and choice. Nobody lives neutrally. Our actions are the result of what we

*Martin Buber, *Two Types of Faith*, Harper & Row, New York, 1961.

consider important. Everyone looks at life in his own way. Everything that we do is in accord with our philosophy of life. Everybody has his own philosophy but many people do not realise this. They do not even think about it, much less go deeply into it. What they do, they do automatically, and consider it to be normal.

Believing family life

Many parents are not aware that they and their family live in a particular way. If this is the way of believing people, whether they are aware of it or not, then the child acquires a faith dimension in all his actions from his earliest years. He drinks it in with his mother's milk.*

From child psychology we learn that the child receives his deepest impressions in early years. Children learn to believe or not to believe at home, and the education which parents provide is the most important. They really are the primary educators in the faith. They do not merely give the child a number of established concepts and behaviour patterns by order of the church. What they teach their child is their own way of believing, their life with God. It is their own particular way of looking at life and acting accordingly.

Many parents know that things vary from one home to another, but as far as their faith is concerned they believe that they are doing the same as all other catholics. These days we hear of other opinions but the people who hold them are not considered good catholics. This reduces faith to a number of outward observances. These could be taught to the children by a priest or the teacher at school. But again we repeat: this is not what faith is all about. Faith is concerned with the whole of life. Believing with your family is your unique way of living with your family. It is a totality of values which parents experience in their own way with their children; it is their life before God. Faith no longer points to the church or religion but to a scale of values, a philosophy of life. This applies to all people. Each family life is based on a specific philosophy of life. For everyone of us, therefore, our own home is a bit different from anyone else's. Our home is that totality of

*Sophia Fahs, *Today's Children and Yesterday's Heritage: a philosophy of creative religious development*, Beacon Press, Boston.

circumstances where we feel like a fish in water. We are not conscious of it ourselves. We notice it only when we visit someone else; their home smells different, sounds different, they do things differently, have things arranged differently, speak somewhat differently. We do things our way. It doesn't have to be this way, and the people next door do it a different way. It just happens to be this way in our house. So we like it better here. We have a reason for it, but often we are not aware of it. If a child asks "Why is this, Mom? Why must it be like this, Dad?" then an adult is inclined to answer: 'Child, don't argue! That's just the way it is."

Yet this is a key question which parents must not evade all the time. Now and again they must put the question to themselves, especially when it concerns matters of vital importance. Why do I do it this way? Why do I still consider this to be so? What is it based on? Why do I get annoyed if my older children do not take any notice of it? If they try to put this into words many things will become clear to them in their mutual relationships. Not to know "why" straight away is not bad at all if they then go searching together and do not just drop the whole issue.

Are they perhaps afraid that if they examine things something very precious will be lost; that the atmosphere, the homeliness, the warmth, the happiness, will suffer? Have they the feeling that in serious matters, the light is going out? If so they are probably close to what we would call the flame of faith which lives in that family.

The first questions to which answers must be found are: Is this really so? Is something precious really being lost? Why do I attach so much importance to it? Just because I learned it that way, and am accustomed to it? Or because it is concerned with the deepest mysteries of life; with God, as the ground of our existence?

Parents cannot just pass these questions and the search for the answers on to the school or the priest. The suggestion: "Ask your teacher or the priest", is no solution because neither teacher nor priest knows exactly what these parents mean by this nor why they act in this way. It is a personal area and the teacher as an outsider can have little or nothing to say. You cannot explain these questions with generalisations because they are based on personal motives and decisions. The flame of faith which lives in a family has its own nutritive source. But it must continually feed from that source. If parents do not want to be bothered any more, if they do not seek for answers along with their "troublesome questioning" children, then the light of faith goes out in that family. The light goes out and they sit in the cold darkness. For the children there is no longer a home where happiness can be found because their parents are not building on firm ground but on loose sand. They have changed their philosophy of life. The school cannot help, for the living experience of faith is lacking.

Religious education in the family

If a family lives in an attitude of faith (for the most part unconsciously but now and again consciously) then the parents will ask what they must do about the religious education of their children.

This too is, in our opinion, something of which all believers are capable. Something they are in fact doing every day, and for which they need no special training. Faith education in a family takes place continuously. It is the meeting in faith which takes place daily in the relationships between all the members of the household.

The simplest folk often do it best.

It may in fact need to take place more consciously today because a number of the crutches which previously supported the life of faith have fallen away: family prayers, the rosary, Friday abstinence, Lent, feast days of saints, May and October devotions, practically all devotions, statues and holy pictures.

The equipping of parents, family catechesis, aims in the first place at giving old and young a little push in the right direction, so that they can acquire the art of more consciously expressing in their family the encounter of faith. We want to show them a way by which they can enter into dialogue with each other, about their own actions and thinking, their value-judgements, and their philosophy of life as Christians. And how they, as parents, can explain something of it to others, to their own children. In fact, it is a matter of learning to speak the language of wonder and reverence again.

Family catechesis does not first demand a certain standard, it lays down no requirements but it does give confidence. It deliberately takes the line of "Parents, you are O.K. You can do it!''*

In this religious education in the family, the first concern is to deal explicitly with what is already there, the mystery underlying everything.

Their first manual is not a file or a book, nor is it scripture. It is the book of their own lives, their own experiences with their children, their own life history. (That is why making a family album is such a fruitful aid.)

And once again: it is a task for all believers, it is their right and even their duty, based on their baptism and confirmation through which they share in the priesthood of the faithful. If they are not yet ready for this, those responsible for the believing community must help them.

But we must be continually on our guard not to give the impression that anything out of the ordinary is required.

This religious education begins in the cradle and proceeds spontaneously throughout the whole parent-child relationship. It is seen in the way parents make the world safe for their children, the example they set them, their wonder, their appreciation, their gratitude, their care, their trust in life and in the people around them. They see it as a gift of God and as an invitation.

Stories play a great part here.† (In the early years stories from life even more than Bible stories). Small children love stories. They come alive every time they are well told. Children recognise in them their deepest feelings. They see themselves as the main characters. At bedtime a prayer linked with the moral of the story is very suitable . . . Not moralising, but indicating how we as believers look at what was told about good and evil, darkness and light, anxiety and joy, and how we then direct ourselves to God who is light and safety, joy and life to us. This is where home liturgy begins! If children have not learned in this way the religious language of life, they will enter a church like a cat entering a strange warehouse. But if they are gradually introduced to it at home, at a given moment, they are ready to join the community of faith ("old enough to go to church") and the family simply needs the additional religious education from the community as well. Without participation in a parish community,

*Thomas A. Harris, *I'm OK. You're OK. How to live and let live.*
†J. B. Metz, 'A Short Apology of Narrative', *Concilium* (English edition), 1973-5, pp. 84-98.

without belonging to the church, we do not see any hope for this life of faith.

Through family catechesis we have reached the firm conviction that the church, that is the parish itself, like the school, has a special educational task in regard to adults as well as to children.

We hope we have made it clear that religious education in the family is something quite different from playing school. It is a special task with a special content, separate from and additional to what happens to the children at school.

*A community of faith which
does not know how to pass
on to its youth the flame
that burns in its midst is
bound to grow old.*

22. THE SECOND MILIEU OF FAITH

As the child grows and makes wider contacts the parish community is the next place where he can learn to believe. It is the
second milieu of faith, because in the parish there is the same
unity of life and purpose as in the family. This can no longer
be said of the school.

Lately there has been a welcome development in church life:
we are beginning to take the children seriously again.

This renewed interest in children in parishes is to be of vital
importance for the continuation of the church. It can lead to the
rejuvenation of the believing community.

In our opinion, it is the only possible form of rejuvenation,
from within.

Parents see how important family catechesis is for them, when
we point out to them that they are missing the chance of a lifetime
to remain young and to grow in faith with their children, if they
neglect their religious education or farm it out to others. The same
thing applies to an even greater extent, to the community of
faith. A believing community which does not know how to pass on
the flame in its midst to its youth, a community which thinks it
can leave this to the schools and the specialists, loses its power to
attract. It becomes estranged from its own young people and must
of necessity grow old. We have only to look about us to see how
true this is.

At one stage we gave the impression that liturgy was an adult
affair, something by adults for adults. The gatherings had to be
real gatherings of mature believers. Consequently all the trimmings such as rows of altar-boys, flower girls, processions,
devotions and sentimentality, all the entourage and frills had to
disappear. In the liturgy, emphasis was placed on the verbal

156

aspect, with themes to cultivate awareness of our world, to increase our sense of responsibility, to make us socially conscious and politically committed. This, of course, had its positive side. It was high time that Christians paid attention to these things. But in the meantime, the children not only stepped quietly away from the altars and the choirs, but they disappeared from the church altogether.

Now a decade later, the aging of the parish community is beginning to show quite distinctly and threateningly. Those who still come to church are growing old together. And then what? Adults without children have no future.

Their place of honour restored

We dare to state categorically that an exclusively adult liturgy never did exist in the catholic church; nor, for that matter, a liturgy exclusively for children. In the early christian community children held a prominent place. They took first place at the sacraments. In the body of the church a special part was reserved for them, not to keep them quiet, but so that they could take an active part as singers and readers, could lead in prayer and participate in the dramatisation of the liturgy. Right up to the time when we were young, the liturgy always had, one way or another, a feeling for the child.

Now we see to our sorrow that for the most part children just tag along in the Sunday liturgy. They obviously do not belong there anymore. No account is taken of them. As a result they are bored and many think nothing can be done about it. As soon as the children can decide for themselves, they stop going to church. And nowadays that happens when they are quite young.

After doing family catechesis for a while we discovered the fundamental importance of liturgy for the living experience of faith, and therefore for the religious education of young and old... Not as a lesson, but as a happening.

After the parents' evenings, parents want to pass on to their children the riches which they themselves have acquired. But they do not know how to do it. They cannot find the right words. The child does not co-operate. They can try for weeks without much apparent result. Then comes the celebration of the theme for the month and it becomes evident that something has got across to the child after all. The child recognises himself in the celebration. After that all kinds of possibilities open up. Children never tire of talking with their parents about all they have seen, experienced and gone through together in the celebration. Then they want to know more and keep on asking questions. From the reaction of parents it is quite clear that what succeeded most were those liturgies in which there was activity and participation. This is true for every occasion when parents and children celebrate together. As one parent said: "Because the family Mass, the christening, the penitential service were feasts for the children, they contributed much and helped to make the parents' task easy."

"Does it all get across to the children?" In other words, "do they understand it all? . . . I think they are still too young for that" another parent said: "He thought the Palm Sunday celebration was wonderful. He certainly wants to go to church." But on ordinary Sundays these same parents are at a loss. This has convinced us that generally there are still shortcomings in our liturgy.

Church attendance continues to decline. An ever increasing number of people do not find the Sunday service to their liking any longer.

Many church-goers do not look forward to who will be present at church — God and their fellow-believers in Christ. They are only aware of what happens there.

23. THE SUNDAY LITURGY

'On Sundays I go to church to meet God, to find some trace of Him once more in my life and in the world, amidst the dull routine of every day. That we do it together encourages me because there are others like me. We render a service to each other through seeking together, mourning together, worrying about one another, sharing joy and surprise. I think it is good to proclaim this together, to pray, to sing and also to hear it told, and to be addressed in the depth of my being . . .' These are the words of someone who experiences the liturgy precisely as it should be; the public worship of the community: service to God through service to each other.

Tracking God down

Good liturgy is always a movement around a central reality: around him who is the centre of our gatherings: God. This takes place through forms, symbols, prayers, narrations, gestures. But these things are only secondary. They do not capture God. They do not formulate God for me in exact terms. They never make God himself visible to me, or close enough to touch.

They are like doors and windows which, when they open before us and we succeed in looking through them, give us an insight into what it is all about: the mystery in our lives which we call God.

The doors and windows are in the first place the living people around us, their part in the circle, their movements and actions. But for a long time now many church-goers have not experienced this. They have no awareness of who is present, but only of what happens there.

And the windows and doors, viz. the forms and rites, have not opened for a long time for many of the faithful. How many have even forgotten what it is all about, that the purpose behind it is a meeting with God?

In all religions we find the same kind of making absolute of external forms among the majority of followers. In others we call this superstition, but if we use the word to our fellow believers, they are deeply shocked.

Losing the trail

We can scarcely blame ordinary laymen if they lose the trail. In recent years they have experienced nothing but alteration to the furniture and fittings: the vernacular, beat music, the altar facing the people, communion in the hand. The doors and windows are perhaps being hung differently on the hinges; at first they only opened inwards, now they can open inwards and outwards.

So much is made of the human forms of expression and their alteration, and so much attention, time and effort is devoted to modernising the surroundings that the ordinary believer inevitably gets the impression: this is still what it is all about in our church.

The great majority experience the liturgy in quite a different way from that described in our first paragraph above.

All the efforts and successive renewals have failed to sustain the interest of the people, they stay away in ever increasing numbers. The Sunday liturgy means little or nothing to many adults.

And for the young people the renewal of the forms of expression is going too slowly. They come to the conclusion that the church is the most boring place in the world, where you hear sermons in out-dated language about people who are long dead and where you sing hymns from ages past. It is a one-man show. If you want to come in you must leave your creativity outside and if while you are inside you feel the desire to tackle something creative, then you must get out in order to do so.

Most people fail to realise that everything that happens on Sunday is not about what can be seen and heard but is actually about the depth-dimension of existence within ourselves and others, about the living God, present here and now, in our midst. One gets the impression that these people do not even have an inkling of this.

Celebration of life now

Liturgical celebration is not about the past. It is never merely a remembrance. It is not a memorial service. It is not a worn-out story about an encounter between people and God in times long past. It is like a good story that you hear again and again and really enter into, not only in your imagination, as if it were happening to you, but in reality: it is happening to you now. Good liturgy is a new encounter with the living God now. It means that on each occasion we experience Jesus among us anew in the various moments of his life. Here and now he makes his presence felt in the deep warmth of our being together as a believing community. Or do we in fact not really believe that he is actually risen, is alive and present to us!

Many believers do not experience anything of this any more. There is an explanation for this: much too little is done on Sundays about the preaching and liturgy of the *here and now*.

Many preachers direct our thought to the future. It used to be heaven, now it is the kingdom that is to come, the better world. Others continually point back to the past. They give the impression that they are concentrating all their efforts on getting across to us how the story of God's dealings with his people must be read and interpreted.

Faith, however, is neither escape from the present, nor losing ourselves in planning for the future, for a church of the future. Nor is our faith an interpretation or reinterpretation of the past.

Liturgy is not a remembrance but a commemoration along the lines of: 'Remember man what you are, that you are dust, that you are now at the table of the Lord, that you are at this moment gathered here together as believers around the Lord.'

Faith for us is looking with other eyes at reality and seeing everything in the light of this mystery, experiencing depth in contact with everything and everyone.

Expressing this in the community is liturgy. But how many of us church-goers still have a feeling for this? How few pastors are really aware of the living mystery here and now, of this divine mystery, while they are occupied with the liturgical actions?

World conditions are vaguely referred to, but not placed in context. The ritual is solemnised in new forms and songs but the doors and windows remain tightly closed to the congregation scattered here and there in the church building.

'It's all very nice, but it is of very little help to us *here and now*' is the complaint of many church-goers. Others put it this way: 'They have so much to say about celebrating: celebrating baptism, celebrating reconciliation, celebrating the eucharist. But there is so little to celebrate. There is so little joy and good news!'

Liturgy is something you celebrate

In spite of everything we consider 'Liturgy is something you celebrate' an apt description and one which we would like to retain.* This means of course that you do not celebrate if there is nothing to celebrate, not even liturgy. You cannot celebrate the liturgy just because it happens to be Sunday and therefore it is prescribed.

Celebrating the liturgical corresponds in this aspect with all other celebrations. There must be an experience of richness, of joy, of some actual circumstance, which calls for celebration even in situations of grief or worry. Liturgical celebration must be related to the good things of our *present* life; the personal life of each participant *now*.

Therefore liturgy involving children must be related to the life of this group of adults and their children.

It is not enough to pay particular attention to children now and again, a special word, or a short sermon. This does not solve anything. The celebration, as such, must have a relevance to the lives of old and young alike. It must be the celebration of their lives. If grown-ups genuinely celebrate, children are certainly no problem. They really enjoy it. They join in automatically.

Now we see children demonstrating by their behaviour that the Sunday liturgy does nothing for them. It does not touch them

*Harvey Cox, *The Feast of Fools*, Harvard University Press, 1969.

at all. It means nothing to them and they show it. Children cannot do otherwise. They cannot pretend or mask their feelings as adults do. Don't they count any more? Don't they belong? Very well then, if they are just going to be bored they won't want to go to church any longer.

This has become so common nowadays that we have become alarmed about it. We have high hopes that the children will open our eyes. We may yet be thankful to them for it. They don't hesitate to call out: 'It's all a farce. There's nothing really there... the emperor has no clothes on!' Then we burst out laughing because we had actually noticed this same thing but nobody wanted to be the one to say it out loud.

The children show their rejection quite openly. But some adults, those who could not bear to go to church on Sundays any longer, have been showing the same thing for a long time. We have maintained that this was laxity, stupidity and bad will on the part of such people. Yet even those who remain faithful have to concede that on Sundays they are not really satisfied, though they do not stay away. 'You persevere. You don't just give up, do you? You can't just throw everything overboard!'

We must be grateful to these persistent ones. But now it is high time for all of us to understand the distress signals which the children are sending out. They are the distress signals of the adults, our own distress signals. This shifts the problem. It is evident that the implications are broader — the liturgy itself is involved.

Shortcomings

The Sunday liturgy is no longer the celebration of a mystery of faith of which we have experience. If we make a list of all the short-comings noted above, we get a shock ourselves: there is too little group experience as a community, too little experience of the mystery and reality of God's presence. It is not an experience of life now: not joyful, creative, inspiring enough, not a genuine meeting of the community of faith. It does not have sufficient relevance to the deepest problems of people, it is too verbal, too cold, too cerebral, too exclusively the action of one man or just a few people.*

*Harvey Cox, *The Seduction of the Spirit*, Simon & Schuster, New York, 1973.

All these faults are real even if they do not all occur simultaneously. They do explain why children opt out completely. Children are the most sensitive to what is wrong here. They are the most vulnerable. They are therefore the first casualties. Children must not become what we adults are now, but we must become as children if we want to find the way back to a living celebration of our faith.

People who set themselves to do something about this (and happily they are increasing in numbers) do good work for all of us. There is in fact no cause for despair. The wonderful thing is that all these shortcomings disappear at one blow once people are able to celebrate in a meaningful way a mystery of faith, which touches their lives. And there the children are no problem at all: they join in, think along, sing along, laugh along, cry along, and pray along.

*Besides the personal
responsibility of parents for
their own children, there
exists a communal
responsibility of all
parishioners for the religious
education of the children in
their midst.*

24. INTERACTION

In many parishes all sorts of things are organised for children
on Sundays: parallel services, children's Masses, family Masses,
family celebrations with dramatisations, mystery plays, creative
expression, singing, music, dancing.

As a temporary solution these are presumably quite all right.
We have everything to relearn.

But there are dangers here. Families are offered another
opportunity of palming off the religious education of their children,
because the school is doing less; and faith and religion are being
made 'childish'.

The end product is not always liturgy. If you start doing these
things immediately, in services for the whole community, there
may be no scope or atmosphere left for a real religious experience.
And faithful churchgoers (especially older people) may not be
able to appreciate it. People need time to adjust. A liturgy for
adults and children together is not out of place. People who are
wholeheartedly involved in it seem to know how to arouse in
children more joy and a positive inclination for going to church
on Sundays, but they also find ways of making these liturgies
real group experiences where everyone feels: God is in our midst.

Initiation

We are convinced that the solution to the problem of liturgy with
children and their participation in the gatherings of adults must
be sought in the initiation of these children into the community
of believers. First of all this must be undertaken by the community
itself. The personal inspiration and convictions of the local com-

munity can only be handed on to the children by the members themselves. Moreover, this must link up with the initiation into the christian life of faith which takes place in the family. The two are mutually dependent. Wim Al says: 'A child can only experience church liturgy as religious formation if he has experienced formation with father and mother at home.' On the other hand 'being preoccupied with children's liturgy at a church level is putting the cart before the horse, if we do not extend a helping hand when it comes to home liturgy'. For some people his language may be off-putting, but family liturgy gives a unique shape to the dimension of family life. It becomes a genuine 'home of learning' where the child learns how to live as a Christian in the course of everyday events. But it must not turn into 'playing at church'.

This interaction between parish and families does not exist, so it will have to be created. People who are concerned about the children of the parish are looking in the wrong direction if they limit themselves to celebrations in church, and seek solutions by improving performance and format or devising novelties. They are on the wrong track if they do not know how to help parents and children within the family to give expression to the religious dimension of daily life.

The specific task of the community of faith

Many co-workers for the children's services see all this falling on them. They are prepared to do something about children in church on Sundays, but must they now take something else on their shoulders? Parents will not be interested. They never co-operate.

These are common reactions, but they reveal a number of presumptions and rash judgements. What really matters is not the kind of beautiful celebrations they can arrange but whether they can be of service to their fellow believers and the children.

If we ever hope to get away from the idea that faith and religion are just fringe phenomena for one short hour per week; if we want people to understand that faith is a dimension of our whole existence and of our actions, we must not get worked up about how and what we are going to do this Sunday. We must put the Sunday liturgy for children into the wider context of relationships in their real lives. Liturgy for one hour on a Sunday has no future at all. If it is true that the child can only become fit for Church liturgy when he has experienced home liturgy, then we see it as a task of the believing community not only to refer to what is happening at home but to offer a service to families to get home liturgies going. A number of parishioners will have to show concern for the families in their midst and be willing to help them. Only then will liturgy with children become possible in the church community.

A broad pastoral offer

Family masses or family celebrations come closest to the ideal.

By these we mean services which from beginning to end can be experienced by young and old as a genuine liturgy in a language understood by all, and in which considerable active participation is possible, by old and young. So it is not an infantile liturgy!

Many parishes have a work-group which prepares and organises the family services. This, of course, is only a small group. So there is the danger that the services could become a performance or a production. This should be avoided. Another danger is that the families remain passive and uninvolved.

If these church celebrations are to be fruitful the work group must help the families so that they are prepared at home to enter into them. This is not an impossible task. The theme of the celebration could be announced in the parish newsletter ahead of time. Suggestions could be made for home preparations: making things, drawing pictures, hanging things up, pasting in pictures, saying prayers, reading bible stories.

It would be even better to draw up a work sheet for the next celebration and give it to parents and children in advance, so that they could think about it or even compose a home liturgy on the theme. The children will then recognise the service in the church more clearly and experience it as a celebration and a confirmation of what they have experienced at home during the week.

Parish catechesis

This all sounds unreal to the ears of some people, but in our opinion, it is one of the secrets of family catechesis. Everything happens with comparative ease. We deal with a number of families who, in the course of a year's catechetical process, become steadily more involved and for whom the celebrations become far more direct. Our catholic celebrations are above all sacramental happenings. Family catechesis is quite decidedly a sacramental catechesis: sacramental in the sense of life hallowing. In this catechesis, before we celebrate a sacrament in church, we begin it at home. This catechesis invites families to give expression to the contents of the mystery of life: first of all in the life of each one individually (in their mutual relationships), and finally in the life of the whole parish. Through a process of thought and action an active core group emerges and becomes a sort of basic community within the parish.

A family liturgy becomes a real celebration of a lived mystery of faith, when parents and children work and grow together at home.

It means even more than that. Quite unobtrusively it radiates out to others, in the parish and beyond it, to "outsiders" young and old, who gladly come and join in the celebrations.

It also means that the themes no longer need to be haphazardly chosen. Life themes considered during the project can be celebrated and even people who went through them the previous year need not regard them as repetitions but as a deepening of the experience. In liturgy personal activity is not only celebrated but also given religious expression, and a deeper experience and understanding of God can follow. Families who participated the previous year will readily give their support and assistance. There are many possibilities and they all serve to build up the church.

Incorporated again

These developments are opening up ways for the greater participation of children in ordinary week-end liturgy in the parish community.

The possibilities are many: a children's choir sings one of the hymns; a child does a reading or makes a personal petition during the Prayer of the Faithful; he helps to prepare the altar. To become an altar boy or girl is again becoming one of the sought after activities, that can entail carrying the gifts, the flowers, forming a procession, or lighting the candles. Children can perform a short play or mime, they can dance, or play music based on the theme of the Sunday; they can hold or carry illustrations, or explain posters displayed at the back of the church.

If in this way, the concept of 'altar-server' is extended and deepened to mean assistant at the service of word and table, whole groups of children could be liturgically involved. With the help of a few creative adults both the children and the Sunday liturgy will benefit.

The preparatory meeting during the week could, at the same time, become a form of parish catechesis.

We must be careful that we do not merely use these activities to make the Sunday celebration more varied and attractive, i.e. not to use them with the ulterior motive of getting adults and their children to church. In everything we do with and for children in the Sunday liturgy our main concern is to give expression to the religious life of the children in the believing community. It is knowing how to place the religious education of youth in the total pastoral context of the parish so that it becomes a genuine service to families and to children.

Children show the way

Children can be a great help, they save us from saying too much, from making the joyous message more difficult and more complicated. With children everything can be much simpler and more spontaneous. They are far more tolerant. They can also help us to return to the experience of faith and the living of faith, so that we can stop expecting to find it in long laborious treatises about faith or about problems and polemics of a church-political or church-diplomatic nature. Has our gathering for Mass begun to resemble an academic conference on a religious theme, surrounded by expressions from the fine arts, which turn it into a sophisticated gathering rather than a liturgical celebration?

Liturgy is a matter for young and old. Liturgy is us and is all about us. Hopefully children are showing the way. Because of their child and because of his education parents are again waking up to many questions. Perhaps we covered up a number of things, and went along with what appeared to be accepted practice, even against our own conscience. Because of the children, cover-up mechanisms and superficial tendencies are broken down. Because of them we take a look at our lives again. The liturgy deals with ourselves and with the faith which we make tenable for each other, so that we can persevere even against the stream. To celebrate liturgy with children you must be yourself, you must be genuine. Be what you are and do what is humanly speaking inconceivable! Only in this way does the experience of God become possible. But then, that will be our experience.

*Besides training pastors,
pastoral workers and
catechists, a new field of
activity opens up for the
church; the equipping of
parents and parishioners,
pastoral co-workers and
teachers, for their task in
religious education.*

25. TASK SHARING AND TEAMWORK

(*See Table III p.* 171)

In this book we shall not go into detail about the training and mission of religious teachers in schools. This would land us right in the middle of the whole problem of catholic education. There are innumerable publications on the subject and sometimes one gets the impression that there are almost as many opinions as there are publications. It is encouraging however that people, and those in school catechesis in particular, are beginning to see a clear direction.

To conclude this section, we would like to sketch in broad outline possibilities for task sharing and teamwork among (I) the family, (II) the parish; and (III) the school. We shall do this by means of table III on p. 171. Reading horizontally across the columns you can see the characteristics of the three partners, how they relate to each other and share tasks with respect to:

1. people
2. area of concern
3. being together
4. task in hand
5. the right people for the task
6. equipping for the task
7. the experience and practice which this provides.

	I. FAMILY	II. PARISH	III. SCHOOL	
			teachers and pupils inspired by evangelical values	
			A.	**B.**
1. People	believing parents and children life community	community of believers unity of life intention	life community the faith dimension of school life	teaching institute lessons in religion school catechesis
2. Area of concern	living in faith dimension of faith of whole being and living and of everything we do together	faith life of the community faith formation in community — religious expression of the faith dimension — celebration of life	the faith dimension of school life	teaching institute lessons in religion school catechesis
3. Being together	faith happenings meeting in faith	faith happenings meeting of believers	faith happenings meeting of "believers"	educational happenings around religion
4. The task in hand — education in faith	education in faith 1. through all relationships at home 2. by means of one's own words discussing the deepest motives of behaviour process of living	education in faith 1. by living liturgy-celebration of life now 2. by proclamation / A. direct accounting for witnessing with one's own words of one's own inspiration and one's own life in faith, hope and love / B. official witnessing from revelation; — giving of broad lines — having the Good News preached	education in faith broadens and widens faith experience of the family practice of Christian way of life	religious formation on systematic level, and ordered approach to religious data
	in practice	in the manner of the parish: celebrating	practising —— in the manner of the school —— studying	
5. The right people for the task	of every believer (priesthood of the faithful)	of all baptised / of pastors and pastoral (co)workers	of teachers and educators	of the teacher of religion the professional catechist
6. Equipping for the task	family catechesis I communion project II confirmation project	adult catechesis III the project of building up the church / formation of liaison team; by means of — guiding — accompanying	direction, teachers by thinking accompanying	catechetical training
7. Experience and practice	in the house of faith God is present	in the house of prayer God's name is called, God is named	in the school the life of faith is practised so Church can happen there	in the house of learning it can be about God, without God

Table III: Task Sharing and Team Work

1. The people

We can divide those interested in the educational relationships into three groups.

I   *Families.* A believing family is a living community of believing parents and children.

II *The believing community.* A parish is a community of people who wish to live the way that Jesus has made possible. They find each other locally in oneness of life purpose.

III *The school community.* A catholic school is a teaching and living community of teachers and pupils inspired by the values of the gospel which they wish to express in a catholic way within education.

2. Defining the area of concern

I   Everything concerned with *living in faith* belongs to the particular territory of each believer and to his life in relation to people, but more particularly, in relation to other believers. Faith is understood as a dimension of our whole being and life and of everything we do in our association with others. The first milieu, in which this believing association can best be realised, is in the family. Being a believer is then a dimension of family life.

II The special area of the parish is the *faith-life* of the community. By this we understand not so much the individual presence of the believer in the church building, but rather the group happenings; the believing expressions of the dimension of faith in the lives of each one personally and of all together, who make up these local communities of faith. Everything they as a local church signify, both superfically and intrinsically, finds its climax in the liturgy: the celebration of their life of faith.

III The school is always in a somewhat ambivalent situation as it is intended to be an institution of learning but is also at the same time a living community. Whatever theoreticians would like to make of it, it remains a fact that, day in day out, a number of adults and groups of young people spend an

important part of their 'living-time' together. For teachers
and pupils it is their second life milieu. It cannot exclude the
personal faith or philosophy of life of each individual's
existence. Of course faith can be covered up and ignored. In
which case it continues to play its part underground and
furtively dictates the direction, but it is never properly dealt
with. This is the worst crime that one can commit in education.

(a) Faith can be emphasised so that being a believer
becomes a conscious dimension of the entire school life.
One can speak of a catholic school in so far as teachers as
a team strive for this. As a community this school links up
with catholic family life to which it offers its services. Just as
with the family, the school can move 'towards a living church'.
(b) If we focus on the aim of the school as an educational
institution, it has the task of dealing scientifically with
religious forms in society. This belongs to the special terrain
of religious education and school catechesis. These lessons
alone, however, do not 'make' the pupils believers and do
not make the school catholic. State education also provides
lesson time on 'religious trends'. If it is really 'catechesis'
then it deals explicitly with the order that underlies everything.

3. Being together

I Being together in a family is a *faith happening* at its deepest
   level. It is the daily encounter in faith of all the members of
   the household with each other through all their relationships.

II In the parish being together is a *faith happening*. The experience
   and celebration of our faith is the reason why we meet each
   other as believers.

III (a) Being together in, for example, a catholic school, is more
    or less a *faith happening* in so far as this is a dimension of
    the many meetings which all the participants in the school
    life share with each other throughout the whole day long.
    (b) At fixed times within this faith happening there is an
    educational happening which deals with matters of faith and
    religion. It cannot be completely separated from the faith

173

happenings at school. Experience, living and celebration play an important part in education and bring us to the deepest level of encounter in faith.

4. The task in hand

Now that we have outlined the areas and sketched the different situations in which partners in faith-education find themselves, we come to the question: what does this imply for religious education? What is each one's task and responsibility? How do they interact and complement each other?

I   Education in the faith is, in the first place, the inalienable task of the family. What happens here, cannot be taken over by any outsider, cannot be farmed out.

   Education in the faith permeates all relationships which members of a household have with one another. They educate one another through the very process of living as believers. Parents must try to express in their own words what the deeper motives of their thoughts and deeds are; what their value-judgements are; and consciously try to explain 'in the family's own way' to their children their attitude and their philosophy of life.

II   We have called the community of believers the second milieu of faith education. Here too, it happens primarily through the process of living, because the faith-life of each one personally and of all together is expressed in reflection and action and finally in the celebration of life in the living liturgy. When this actually does take place it is precisely this living liturgy which is the most effective religious formation for children. They feel that the liturgy is alive, lives for their parents and for all the other grown-ups. This is the best form of proclamation.

(a) Yet the ritual can too easily become a routine performance of hackneyed gestures if it is not regularly considered in depth and clearly presented to young and old. Believing people can be led to bear witness in simple words to their own faith, hope and love.

(b) Liturgy can also be examined in a formal way through preaching and parish catechesis where we can probe its

174

meaning in depth. Thanks to biblical theology and exegesis this is also the place where the official revelation of God's salvific actions is presented, where the good news is seen as liberation and enrichment in the individual's search for meaning. This official proclamation can only come across as genuine and be effective when preparation in family, parish and school is continuous.

III (a) As far as religious education is concerned, the Catholic school through its daily life is the third milieu where the meeting of believing people takes place.

In the daily routine it continues to build on the practice of living faith which is initiated in the family. Through the school this living is broadened and extended. In this way the school can become a genuine training ground, *a practical living-out of the christian way of life.*

(b) In addition, the school has its own task of giving the youth a well-founded religious formation. This is achieved by dealing "scientifically" with the things of faith and religion in an orderly systematic, way. This involves a more objective approach to religions.

Now we arrive at what many people consider the most important part of religion and catechesis: knowing and understanding the systematic teaching. This is what characterises teaching of religion in schools and parents rightly say that the teacher can do it better than they, because he has been trained for it.

This instruction could be theology, biblical studies, church history, cultural formation or sociology and it can, as we have seen, quite spontaneously move into moments of real faith education.

5. The right people for the task

Good teamwork can be greatly facilitated if there is clarity about who the right people are for a specific task.

I   Religious education takes place in the family in the normal course of events. It happens spontaneously as the need arises or when actions need explanation. This type of religious

175

education is the task of every believer, his right and duty, his part in the priesthood of the faithful. Therefore it is bound to be within each one's capabilities. And because it is about each person's own actions and omissions it cannot be referred to others for explanation.

II (a) To live this out in the community of faith, to give example to the youth, and pass it on to them, is the task of all the baptized. Whoever opts out, fails in his service to the faith-life of others.

(b) It is the specific responsibility of pastors, pastoral workers and co-workers to initiate discussion officially about the basic inspiration which lives in the believing community.

III (a) Religious education at a Catholic school is one aspect of of all its subjects and processes. It is the responsibility of all teachers and more especially of the class teacher, the catechist, and the counsellor (if there is one). What takes place in a particular class, the behaviour of the teacher, his attitude and relationship to his pupils, each one's motives and intentions, especially at particular moments of high tension in their relationships, cannot be explained by any outsider, neither can it be passed on to the priest, for example. Nor is it settled by punishment. On the contrary, when the pupils ask why a teacher says and does a particular thing, he must not brush them off saying 'that has nothing to do with the lesson. Ask the catechism teacher later'. It is his own task as educator in the faith.

(b) Religious formation as a subject is the particular task of the subject teacher in religion or catechesis.

6. Equipping for the task

The church is confronted with a tremendous task and it has hardly begun to meet it: to equip each believer in his own place, for his own task. Such training is the church's responsibility. Only in this way is good teamwork possible among all concerned in religious education.

I Many families do not know what to do about their duty as the first milieu of religious education. They are in need of training

Photo: Michael Shinners

in family catechesis. Parents need help and so do older children. For this reason we have a communion project (I) and a Confirmation project (II).

II (a) There is a great need for adult catechesis, not only to enable people to teach youth and to give witness but also to equip them to act in the name of the church (for example in the neighbourhood and at work) and to offer their services (for example to the sick, the aged etc).

(b) The church has always paid attention to the education of pastors and pastoral workers. But there are still far too few opportunities for other leaders to qualify further. Therefore we have drawn up guides and files for all our projects and offer suggestions and models for pastoral workers in general and for teenage catechesis in particular. The best form of training is, and always will be, the personal guidance of these groups of volunteers. This is a form of adult catechesis which is one hundred percent effective for the believers themselves, and this makes it effective for others.

III (a) Among teachers and organisers there is the same need for guidance and training as there is among the pastoral co-workers. If catholicism is to be an important dimension of school life and of their teaching, then it must find a place on the agenda of their meetings. Room and time will have to be found for this so that they can search together as a team of teachers and enter into discussion with each other in depth, and examine basic issues and values.

(b) Meanwhile different training and guidance possibilities are emerging for professional catechists and teachers of religion, some better than others. All together there is quite a wide field for the church to render service to all concerned with religious education. At present it is mainly a matter of sowing laboriously, and tending, but the harvest promises to be good.

7. Experience and practice which this provides

Finally we would like to sketch some characteristics of the atmosphere in which religious education takes place in the different milieus, and show how they contribute to its experience and realisation.

I   The family becomes a home of faith. There the life of faith simply becomes integrated in the home life of people. God is present there.

II Besides being a house of faith the parish church is even more a house of prayer. There God is called by name. God's name is evoked from the depths of our being: here our speaking, singing and praying stem from life. We call on God and express to others the depth of our existence and we listen attentively to it in one another. That is faith and liturgy and religious education all in one.

III (a) In schools drawing their inspiration from gospel values, the life of faith finds a home and is 'practised'. The Lord is present there.

N.B. When, in this milieu, the personal life of faith comes under discussion people speak from genuine authentic life and experience. They speak to God as the ground of their personal existence. Neither in the family nor in the parish, nor in the school, should committed speech be replaced by talk learned about God or some statement about what God is.

It is more important to be a believer than be able to philosophise about what faith is.

(b) The school has its own task and its own approach: the objective and abstract treatment of reality and life. In school as the house of learning, religion can be treated as a scientific phenomenon. It is possible to teach about God, without God.

Society has many views and opinions on life so it can be important to be able to speak intelligently about God and to be able to philosophise about what believing means. A believer who can carry on a conversation on this level about other things cannot permit himself to fall short in a discussion about religion and faith.

26. FAMILY CATECHESIS : A SUMMING UP

What is family catechesis?

Family catechesis is the equipping of parents so that it becomes clear to them that in living out their daily life with each other and with their children in faith they are developing as a living cell of the church today.

What is new in family catechesis?

Family catechesis gets a dialogue going between the parents of families. Through discussion their task as believers becomes clearer to them. They are the persons primarily responsible for their families.

Family catechesis opens up an area of pastoral and catechetical work which up till now has been largely untouched.

In what way does it differ from other forms of catechesis?

a) Family catechesis does not intend parents to give religious lessons at home. There are other people to do this. It does convince parents, however, that they are the teachers of life and faith in their own family.

b) Family catechesis does not mean doing away with or replacing existing forms of religious education: school catechesis, parish catechesis, adult catechesis and the like. It does make clear, however, where the influence of parents begins and how this is of vital importance to relationships and to systematic forms of instruction.

c) Family catechesis is not a kind of refresher course or an opportunity for adults to discuss modern religious questions. Other forms of adult catechesis provide for that. But as the persons primarily responsible for the religious education of their children, parents face decisions that baffle them. Family catechesis aims at helping them come to decisions.

Who is concerned in family catechesis?

Where does family catechesis take place?

a) Family catechesis *uses* the high points in family life as occasions for reaching out to parents and children: in practice these are the 'sacramental' moment of baptism, communion, confirmation, engagement, marriage.

b) Family catechesis is *initiated* by the parish. For this reason meetings are best held in the parish hall. The central part of these meetings is a meditative catechesis on the theme of the month. It is usually introduced by a priest or a pastoral worker and parents can participate in various ways.

c) The actual family catechesis *takes place* in the family, in the homely atmosphere of daily life and faith.

d) Family catechesis is *celebrated* in the parish and draws its inspiration for daily life from the local community of faith. By this the people's houses become once again the dwelling of God, and God's house becomes once more a dwelling for people.

The 'missing link' in catechetical and pastoral work

The whole concept of family catechesis was born out of a need. It brings faith back to where it belongs in the family. It gives parents back the faith (which many feel has been taken away from them) and the responsibility to live it, in their family, at their own level.

So long as parents are not addressed as worthy and equal partners in this dialogue, no real results can be expected from any higher form of pastoral work, liturgical change, or religious formation.

Dangers and hindrances

Experience with family catechesis has brought to light a few persistent misunderstandings which parents have:
— Many parents still try to palm off their task to the school: "The teacher can do it better. She has been trained for it. It is her job."
— Other parents think that they must now turn the home into a class room.

The real misunderstanding however is that, for most parents, religious education always means explaining things in detail, knowing stories, learning bits of knowledge, giving the right answers. Of course things go wrong if they try this. In fact, children just will not accept it from them.

Religious education in the family occurs through the daily activities of all members of the family together. It is something which believers are normally engaged in, or at least should be. It requires no extra training at all. People must of course be made aware of it.

What are the results of family catechesis?

Family catechesis, tackled in the right way, yields the following results:
a) Children "gladly go to church", live their faith and want to know more about it.
b) Parents, at a given moment, "re-discover their faith" or begin to live it anew with deeper conviction, "become better people" (as they say themselves).
c) Pastoral co-workers emerge from among these parents. They too begin to help with projects.
d) A liturgy develops which is more closely related to people's experience and interests.
e) There is a growing and closer bond of trust between pastor and parishioners through manifold and deeper personal contacts.
f) There is a gradual revival of the entire life of the parish and this inspiration touches all parish happenings.
g) Parishioners develop a sense of belonging; a community spirit grows among members of the local church.

h) There is a renewal and rejuvenation of the community of faith as a real **PEOPLE OF GOD** where every member becomes his brother's keeper.

FAMILY CATECHESIS CATCHES ON AND INSPIRES: IT POSSESSES AN INNER VITALITY, SO THAT IT SPREADS ITSELF SPONTANEOUSLY AND AUTOMATICALLY AMONG THE PEOPLE AND DEMANDS GREATER INVOLVEMENT, GROWTH AND DEVELOPMENT.

APPENDIX I :

An alternative cycle for the Communion Project in the Southern Hemisphere

	I OUR FAMILY (May)	II CHILD IN THE HOME (June)	III SET ON THE WAY (August)
Human Experience	The family is the basic model of communication — the heart of society — mutual: giving — receiving — makes life possible, pleasant, happy — gives purpose to life, to each other, to the child	The child is both gift and challenge to its parents — likewise parents are gift and challenge to their child — entrusted to or at each other's mercy — mystery of passing on of life; birth — living off and for each other gift of love in daily bread — rich in each other; grateful	Birth: the ways of people — becoming human through each other — learning to live in the spirit of a nation, language, laws But: inherited attitude of WE! and THEY! — cause of division, sin, war
Believing Experience	COMMUNION The Christian family is the basic model of Holy Communion — heart of the believing community, of the whole family of God, the whole of mankind Choice of leading children into this community of faith, to let them communicate in Christ	THE FATHER'S HOUSE Being a child of the Father; rich and happy with everyone; grateful for all that is good. Life is a gift of God: Child of God. Good tidings. Father-religion authority God's Son. Praying to God	PEOPLE OF GOD Baptism: the way of God — together journeying on with all others in the spirit of God. — Drawing strength from the source of living water. Religion of brotherhood, Love of neighbour. — Liberation from Original Sin, Ten Commandments, law of love.

IV LIFE & DEATH (September)	V HEALTHY LIFE (October)	VI ETERNAL LIFE (November)
Nature: living and dying: Society: buying. People: consume each other, pass on life. Growth: child "dies" to become an adolescent — adult — leaving things behind in order to move on. — well-being above welfare. — doing justice.	Health is the greatest possession: physical-spiritual unity. Disease of our culture: means before people — poor substitutes in education — obsession which becomes mute or aggressive — ready for doctor, psychiatrist or priest?	Law of life and living off and for each other. Love is: giving oneself as food for others. — human depth of life eating from each other — bread is more than mere food.
SACRIFICE	LAMB OF GOD	THE MEAL
Mortification — dying in order to live, way of life: I am the Way, the Life not standing still, holding on, but letting go, leaving behind (sacrifice) to go further (happiness). Losing oneself for the sake of others and thus finding oneself.	Healing and liberation, redemption — standing still, holding on, is sin — putting things before people, obsession, isolation The Lamb of God takes away sins, requires faith and the will to let go. Healthy faith.	Food for eternal life to be able to go further along the way of God. Love is: giving one's life as food for others. Fulfilment of law of life: eating at source of life: mystery of our faith: Christ our food.

187

INDEX

Abraham, 98
Abstinence, 153
Action, 40
Acts, 40-1
Adults, x, 155, 163
    immature, 95-6
Al, Wim, 166
Authority, 48, 51, 54, 55, 94, 143,
    144

Baptism, 39, 85, 113, 119, 120, 154,
    158, 162
Behaviour norms, 46, 49-51, 52, 54,
    55, 59, 84
Bible, 38, 40, 75, 77, 86, 98, 100,
    111, 130, 144, 167
Bishops, 101
Bluyssen, Mgr, 78
Boerwinkel, 46
Bosco, Don, v, 75, 106
Bournique, 40
Buber, Martin, 150n.
Bulckens, J., 41n.

Caster, Marcel van, 45n.
Catechesis, defined, 38-42
    science and, 86-8
Catechism, 144
Catechists, 40, 49, 87, 179
Children,
    liturgy and, 141, 157-8, 162-9, 174
    parents v., 23, 29, 102, 142-5
    parish and, 21, 156
    society and, 20-1
Christian, being a, 68-9, 85
    humanist v., 76-8
Christmas, 112, 113, 118, 119, 120,
    126, 129, 147
Church,
    attendance, 73, 158

children, youth and, 141, 156, 160
communion in Early, 105
denominations, 67-9
duties of membership, 97
freedom and, 96, 101
house of prayer, 180
priest-centred v. lay-centred, 103, 124
school and, 17, 18, 20, 22
society and, 19, 95
task of, 26, 39, 107, 176, 179
Coincidence, 55-6
Colomb, J., 52n.
Colson, Jean, 66n.
Communication, 146, 147
Communion, 18, 24, 103, 117
    First, *see* First Communion
Communion project, ix
    aim of, 104, 105
    laity in, 93, 124, 133
    materials for, 91
    pastors and, 123-4, 126, 127, 130
    practical work, 93, 115-18, 123-30
    programme, 108-11, 115-19
    result of, 13
    structure of, 93, 106, 120-1
Community, 26, 27, 59, 65-7, 69, 131
Confession, 18, 101
Confirmation, 18, 39, 48, 154, 179
Conscience, 48, 97, 103
I Corinthians, 42
Cox, Harvey, 73n., 162n., 163n.

David, 98
Decision-making, 93, 100-5
Devotions, 153

Easter, 113
Education,
    complaints against, 22
    models of, 51-3
    parent-child in, 142-3

189

Equipping, 146
  aim of, 30, 153
  believers, 176
  defined, 30
  method used, 110-11
  parents, 17, 153
  teachers, 38
Ernst, Mgr, 135
Exeler, A., 65n.
Exodus, 66

Fahs, S., 151n.
Faith,
  family life and, 151-3, 173, 180
  meaning of, 18, 145
  milieu of, 141, 156, 172, 174
  religion and, 141, 150
Family catechesis, 23
  aim of, 17, 28, 31-2, 69, 153, 181-3
  approach to, 30-1, 118
  meaning of, vi, vii, 17, 26-7, 37,
    70, 127
  method of, 141
  parents and, 17, 28-30
  results of, 183-4
Family services, 167
Feast days, 153
First Communion, 119
  family occasion, 107
  parents and, 108-14
  pastoral approach to, 106
  preparing for, 71-2, 93, 104-5, 117,
    142, 143
Freedom, 94-6, 101-2

Galatians, 67
Greeley, A.M., 96n.
Group experience, 56-65

Harris, Thomas A., 154n.
Humanism, 76-8

International Catechetical Conference,
  40

Jehovah's Witnesses, 97
Jesus, 40, 42, 46, 47, 69, 72, 74, 81, 82,
  85, 98-9, 105, 172
Jews, Judaism, 63-5, 82
I John, 111
Joshua, 63-4

Kierkegaard, 55
Kingdom of Heaven, 42, 85, 98
Knowledge, 43-4, 47, 145

Laity,
  Communion project and, 93, 124, 133
  role of, 38-40, 103
  Vatican II and, 39-40
Laws, 52, 54, 94, 101
Lent, 113, 119, 120, 153
Liturgical year, vi, 119
Liturgy, 141, 156-69, 172, 174
  children and, 141, 157-8, 162-9, 174
Luke, 40

Mass, 68, 81, 119, 120, 158, 162, 165,
  169
Matthew, 46, 47, 79, 85
Meditation, 111, 112, 124
Metz, J.B., 154n.
Moltmann, J., 65n.
Moses, 47, 98

Palm Sunday, 158
Parents,
  children v., 23, 29, 102, 142-5
  evening, 93, 110-18, 127
  family catechesis and, 17, 28-30
  First Communion and, 108-14
  religious education and, 17, 21,
    24-5, 28, 29, 31, 38, 144-5, 151,
    153-6, 174
Parent-teachers' associations, 21, 124
Parish, vi, 17, 172, 173
  acceptance into, 107, 109
  aging people in, 157
  children in, 21, 24
  families and, 166
  task of, 110
Parish catechesis, 21, 26-7
Pastor, 179
  Communion project and, 123-4, 126,
    127, 130
  defined, vi
  role of, 24, 30, 131-2, 134-5, 148, 176
'Pastoral', meaning of, 134-6
Pastoral approach, 17, 105-6, 112-14
Pastoral co-workers, 124, 126, 132-4,
  176, 179
Pastoral offer, v., 24-5, 167
Paul, St, 42
Paul VI, Pope, 76
Photographs, 118
Populorum Progressio, 53, 76
Prayer, 18, 110, 112, 153, 157, 159, 180
Preaching, 160, 161, 162, 174
Process, vi, 93, 114, 123, 131-3
Proclamation, 40
Psalms, 81

Reality,
   attitudes to, 82-5
   dimensions of, 79-82, 88
Relationships,
   with God, 55, 70
   with Jesus, 98-9
   importance of personal, 22-3, 41, 52, 84-5
   regulating, 54
Religion,
   faith and, 141, 150
   group experience and, 59-65, 70
Religious education,
   aim of, 48
   changes in, 24
   parents in, *see under* Parents
   partners in, vi, 23
   renewal of, 26
   requirements of, 17
   results of, 180
   school and, 38, 110, 176
   total context of, 18, 175-6
Rome, 40, 101
Rosary, 153

Sacraments, 144, 167-8
   need to experience, 71-3
School,
   catechesis, 23, 26
   Church and, 17, 18, 20, 22

   clergy and, 21
   methods, 146-7
   new ways in, 20-1, 23
   primary, 38
   secondary, 135
   task of, 18, 20, 21, 25, 110, 172-3, 175, 180
Science, 55, 86-8
Second Vatican Council, 39, 40
Signs and symbols, 58-9, 67, 70, 81
Society, 180
   children and, 20-1
   Church and, 19, 95
   forms of, 83
   school and, 22
   secularisation of, 73, 75
Standards, 96-7

Total context, vi, 22

Values,
   behaviour norms, v., 46, 49-50, 51, 52, 54, 55, 59, 84
   Christ as deepest, 100, 111
   education and, 51, 52-3
   eternal, 46, 55, 67, 70, 84-5, 111
   human, 44, 46, 49-50, 55
   swept away, 94

Youth, Church and, 141, 156, 160